With much appreciation

Silent Sinners, Silent Saints

Silent Sinners, Silent Saints

by

Daniel Drubach

Introduction and Storyteller Notes by John Graner

This book is a work of fiction. Names, characters, places and incidents are products of the authors' imaginations or are used fictitiously. Any resemblance to actual events or locales or persons living or dead is entirely coincidental.

Published by GRANDOC PUBLISHING
grandoc@mac.com

Library of Congress Control Number: 2001012345

To order additional copies, please contact
www.booksurge.com

Wholesale orders may be placed at
www.booksurgedirect.com

"We are surrounded by silent sinners and silent saints. They stand within a crowd, and sometimes within ourselves, but they remain so quiet that we cannot hear them. But they are definitely there, and if we listen very closely, we'll know who they are."

Contents

Introduction

I am "the Storyteller." I was born in 1880. It is now 1925. I am sitting in my home in San Diego. I write these basic facts in order to restore to my confused mind some order, some reality. You see friend, I have recently had a most incredible experience, so incredible that I am not exactly sure that I can call it "real." I have heard things that few people have heard, in a way that is absolutely unique, for I have journeyed to a place in which there seems to be no distinction between events and the meaning of those events. At least I think that is what the old bartender was trying to tell me!

Let me tell you a bit more about myself, in order that you may understand how I came to be in that little town, buried somewhere in Central America, from which the strange stories in this volume originated. I have lived most of my life in southern California, but of my beginnings I know little. My skin is dark, and I know that my present parents found me in a poor orphanage in Central America, so I am of Central American stock. It always disturbed me that I did not really know from whence I came.

9

I earn my living as a writer. Some time ago I "ran dry," as writers sometimes do, and had the feeling that I had nothing important to say any more. I decided that there is only one remedy for that; I had to get a sample of stories "straight from the people," as they say. So, I made a trip down into Central America- in exactly which country I don't care to say. I traveled from town to town, getting a flavor for the people- the people who might really be my own. The folks in the little towns started calling me "the Storyteller," because I told them that I was gathering stories for a book I was thinking of writing.

I had been in the area for a few weeks, not feeling particularly "inspired" by what I was seeing, when a little fellow grabbed me by the arm (I wish in the worst way now that I had learned that little guy's name, or at least remembered what he looked like!), and told me that if I wanted to hear stories, important stories, I should travel to a little town called "Recuerdos," a word that in Spanish means "Remembrance." I remember thinking at the time that that was a very strange name for a town, but it sure sounded appropriate for my current needs.

So, off I went to "Remembrance." Once I got there, I have to say that it didn't appear much different to me from the other villages in the area. I did notice that it seemed to have a lot of roads leading into it, though. "Almost like the spokes of a wheel," I remember telling myself as I drove my old car into the place. I found a room in a cheap hotel over the little tavern the old man had told me to visit, and informed the bartender, another elderly fellow, that I would like to hear some stories and that I would pay for good ones. With a knowing look in his eye (or so it seemed to me) he assured me that I would not be disappointed.

I was not prepared at all for what I ended up hearing there. Somewhere, at some point during those interviews, I became "detached" - not just from my immediate surroundings, but from all surroundings. Because it was so unreal, it is very difficult for me to remember that experience- I can't associate it with anything else in my life.

The most vivid aspect of the whole thing was the group of people who told me their stories. They were surreal. They were all so, shall we say, "vivid"- almost "archetypical" in a way. Face it: characters like the "pendulum man" just don't exist in real life! But the last person I interviewed was not only the most vivid, but also the most real. All of this sounds a bit confusing, but if you keep reading you will see what I mean. And the bar itself- there was something strange about the place. I felt almost as if the entire proceedings had been staged for my benefit. And like everyone else, the bartender turned out to be more than he let on to be. I have an idea about him, of who he really was, but I hesitate to believe it. It scares me to think about it!

My thoughts keep returning to the same questions: What made that amazing group of people stand in line waiting to tell me their stories? A simple word from the bartender, and it seems that they appeared out of nowhere. And what stories they told! And in such a strange fashion! My friend, these are stories one does not hear every day; they almost seemed to flow from some deep subconscious place. Hell, when I sat down to transcribe them from my shorthand notes, I even had trouble putting them into simple words!

The reality of the whole thing is my chief concern right now, because if it was real, then there is someone I have to find, or should I say someone who will find me. I can't imagine that this unique group just happened to come into the bar that day, and just happened to all want to tell me the things they did. That's what I mean when I say I feel like the whole thing was staged. And so it all returns back again to those two old men: the fellow who sent me to the town, and the bartender who seemed to be waiting there to greet me.

Did I hallucinate the entire interview process? Did I pass out in the bar and dream it all? The notes that I took tell me otherwise. I know one thing: at the end of the day I had stories to tell; I once again had something to write about. Brother, did I! So, no matter where they came from, these stories are important and should be recorded. I leave it to you, Dear Reader, to make sense of it all! I have done my best to faithfully translate into

SILENT SINNERS, SILENT SAINTS

English what was said to me, while retaining the unusual style and spirit in which those words were conveyed. In that effort I am afraid I have to some extent failed, a shortcoming for which I must beg your forgiveness.

Maria and David

[Storyteller's note: This first story set the stage for that strange day. It was told to me by the only patron already sitting in the barroom when I sat down, a scruffy looking fellow with several drinks too many under his belt. He literally hung on me after I had seated myself beside him. He sat to my left. As he began his mumbling monologue, the line of those with more coherent and planned stories, apparently informed of my presence and procured somehow by the bartender, began to form to my right. Rarely did this little fellow pause even to take a breath, and his entire tale came across as one long sentence. I had a devil of a time keeping up with him, even in shorthand!]

The bartender assures me that you are looking for stories, and he even told me that you may pay me well; that is, if you like the one I tell you, but even if you do not pay me, you can at least buy me a few drinks; that is, again if you like my stories, but let me tell you that having lived here for an infinity, I know an infinite number of stories, all of them true I may add, because even though this is a small town, and people will tell you that nothing ever happens here, in reality everything happens, because everything happens everywhere, and also the strangest things, but I have to wonder why you, a writer, why you would need stories from other people, because I always thought that writers made up their own stories, or wrote what they observed, because writers have imagination, and I know, because there was a time, or I really mean many times, when I also wanted to write, but I'm no writer; I hardly know how to speak well, and in recent years even speech has been leaving me, to the point that I have become very quiet, not totally by choice I may add, because if someone listens, like you are listening to me now, I may be more of a speaker, but that is the problem these days- everybody wants to speak, and therefore there's nobody to listen. That's why I don't really mind if you don't pay me, although I hope you do, because God knows I need the money; but if you listen, that would be enough, that is, if you buy me drinks, because lately I can't even afford drinks, even though they are cheap in this bar; that is, if you buy the house liquor, although you have to be used to it, or else it will make you sick, because I believe the owner makes the alcohol, so it's not too good, because he doesn't care, like everyone here- no one cares for anybody else, and I shouldn't speak, 'cause I'm the same- now, that is- because I wasn't like this, and the way you're looking at me, the way I am dressed, I can tell what you are thinking, that I'm a drunkard, a broken man- and you are right, I am just

what you think, that is, in my heart, because I'm broken; I have lost it all- have nothing left to lose, because
if I were not a shattered man I wouldn't be here, in this
forsaken place, the end of the world, a place in the
wind, where there's always wind, too much wind- wind
which blows the dust until it covers the sun. Although I
still don't know why you are here- to collect stories I
am told, but you look like a distinguished man- from the
city perhaps- and I don't know why you would come
here to collect stories when there are probably so many
more in the city, although like I told you before, everything happens here, but you are lucky that you found
me here, that is, because if you hadn't found me, nobody else would have told you anything; stories that is,
because people here don't know any, or don't remember, people here just like to forget things, they don't
have memories, they bury their dead and they just cry a
little, those who cry that is, and then they forget the
dead person, like if they hadn't existed, and perhaps
that's a good thing, because if you are able to forget,
that is, the bad things, then you will not feel the remembrance pains, as I call them, and I should know, because I have them all the time; and even though they
say that alcohol will make you forget, that is, it will
cause you to lose your memory, but I drink a lot, and I
guess I have forgotten a lot, but not the bad memories,
and I still suffer from remembrance pain, a deep pain,
that not even the cheap liquor here can drown, but I
guess that you are not interested in me, that is, you
want me to tell you the story, and by the look on your

face I guess you think I talk too much, but I am a quiet
man, like I told you; that is, but only because people
don't listen, and now you are listening and I am talking,
because one fits the space he is given, and when there
is no space, one remains cramped, unable to move, one
cannot expand, and I guess I must thank you, you are
giving me room, and that's an important act of kindness
too little practiced, to give others room, and thus when
there is someone to listen I become a big talker, and
when no one listens I am quiet, so much that I sometimes become fearful, although I am not a fearful man,
but everyone has his fears, even you I can tell, but
that's none of my business, although people say that too
much, so that no one worries about anybody else; that
is, not because they don't care, but because it's none of
their business, and I know they don't try too hard to
make it their business, and it's so unclear, what is and is
not your business and like I was saying, sometimes I
don't say a word for days at a time; that is, except
when I come to the bar, and even then I don't say much,
'cause I just drink and when I don't have money for
drinks I just sit but don't say anything, and I come just
for the company, because the remembrance pains are at
their worst when you are alone, because when one is
alone then one becomes too silent, and people here say
silence is good, but that is only because they have lost
their memory, but I still have my memory, and when I'm
too silent I begin to remember and I get the pain, so I
come to this bar, and the bartender lets me sit, and
sometimes he feels sorry for me and gives me a free

drink, but not too often; but when I am too quiet, that is for days at a time, like I told you, I become fearful that I have forgotten how to talk, and then I scream out loud, that is, when I am by myself, because people here they don't talk much, like I told you, and I don't know how they would react if I would scream; that is, if I had no reason, because if I had a reason they would probably try to help me; that is, if it didn't require much helping, because even though they are good people they are always quiet, and sometimes they seem to act as though they were atoning for a sin, one that they committed a long time ago, but it happened so long ago that now they have forgotten the sin, and only remember how to atone, which brings me to my story- that is, to the story I want to tell you, because I can tell you think I talk too much about myself, although I am a quiet man, but if you think about it we always talk about ourselves; that is, even when we talk about something else, even though we don't want to admit it, or we can't see it. But, going back to my story, it happened long ago; that is, if it ever happened at all, because I remember the story, but not how I heard it, that is if I heard it, because things that really happened become confused over time with things you heard, and you can't tell the difference between the two, and it could be that I heard the story, or that it happened to me or someone I know, or even that I dreamt it; that is, when I used to dream, because now I don't dream much, and like I was telling you, this story happened a long time ago, when I was a young man, because even though I see disbelief in your eyes, I was young once, and not too long ago, though you may not believe it, I haven't been old too long, if it wasn't for the silence, and the memory pains, and the loneliness too, which I haven't talked about, because I talked about too many sad things, and now even with this story, which I am about to tell you, and sadness shouldn't be added to sadness, and thus I won't mention the loneliness, that is, at least not now; but anyway this is a simple story, perhaps too simple for your liking, that is, because I haven't read much, but I have heard about stories that are written, and you writers like complicated stories, but the real stories are simple, and perhaps after you heard it, you won't want to pay me, but that's all right, cause you are buying me drinks, and you are listening to me, and I haven't talked in such a long time, and this is a simple story anyway, and perhaps you heard it many times before, but you have never heard it from me, and anyway, if I don't tell you this story, nobody else in this town would tell you another one, and then you would have wasted a trip, that is if you really came here only to listen to stories, because I have been here many years, and the only people that ever come here are those that have needed to atone, for a sin they remember or most often have forgotten, for this is like that city in the Bible, where people who had committed a crime came for safety, only that here you are never safe from yourself, because there is too much silence. But you are a writer and chose to come here, although one never chooses anything without a reason, but the reason is hidden; that is, even from ourselves, but you look angry and rightly so, and I hope you will forgive me for speaking about your business, but I haven't spoken for so long and you have been kind enough to listen and buy me drinks, and you know that the alcohol loosens the tongue, and I am talking too much, even though I am a quiet man. And to get back to the story, which may be too simple for your liking, it happened in a town close to here, and in this town in the story there was this boy named David, an unworthy name, because David, the real David that is, the one in the Bible, was a strong courageous man, but the one in the town was insecure, and perhaps a coward, and anyway, they shouldn't give people other people's names; that is because they may be better or worse than the one before them, and therefore they should give people fresh new names, so that they won't have somebody to live up to; but to go on with the story, David grew up in a home of modest means, but in a town where everybody was poor, David's family was rich, and they had a servant woman, a hard working, honest but quiet woman, and this woman had a daughter named Maria. That is not an original name, because half the girls in this town were named Maria; but she, unlike David, deserved the name, and Maria and David were of the same age and grew up together, and everyone could tell that they were fond of each other, and David's father took him aside one day, or many days, and explained the differences between them, that is, between David and Maria, and David understood, and told it to Maria, who only listened, because when David

talked Maria listened, but no one else did because David
was not too bright; that is, he wasn't dumb but he was
very insecure, and they grew up, and when it came time
to leave the town, for David to go to school, Maria cried
but didn't say much and she waited for the summers
when he would come home, and then she would listen
to his stories, like you are listening to me, 'cause no
one else listened, and with time, and when he went
away, in the beginning, he would write to Maria, but
only in the beginning, 'cause then he met new friends,
but when he came back one summer Maria confessed to
him that she loved him, and he said he loved her too,
that is, he only said it, because he did not love her, or
didn't think he did, and they made love that night and
other nights, and after making love David would talk,
and Maria listened like no one else listened, and David
never stopped to think what it meant for a girl in this
small town to lose her virginity, because he had never
planned to marry her, even though he loved her; or
more likely, he needed her to love him, because cowardly men, and many not so cowardly, desperately need
a woman to love them, but he never stopped to think,
and then he went away, but not before implanting a
seed in Maria which grew into a woman child, and when
David found out he said nothing and neither did Maria,
that is, she never told anybody in the town it was his
child, even though people suspected, and when one
summer he came back home and Maria told him, he
laughed and asked her how she knew that it was his,
and this caused a terrible pain for Maria, almost like a

knife in her heart, but she said nothing, just looked at David, and he felt terrible inside for saying what he said but did not apologize, and that kept happening during his entire life- that is, him saying things he didn't want to say, and him feeling sorry afterwards but never apologizing, not because he was a bad man, but an insecure one, and perhaps a coward, and insecurity and cowardice can be terrible things, because in the end it turns you into a bad man, and one who is insecure should do his best to overcome it, but he never could, even though he tried his best, and after he said what he said to Maria she never talked about the child to him, never asked for anything, nor did he ever offer or ask, but she continued to love him, that is, her love did not decrease until the day of her death, because to her love was sacred, and of truly sacred things there is only one, and therefore she never loved any other man, although many loved her, but she wasn't able to love them back, that is, she tried a few times, because it was hard for a lonely woman and a lonely child to survive, but she never could, and additionally she told the truth, that is, to those who loved her she told the truth, that she couldn't love them. And now I realize, but I didn't then, that David loved her back, perhaps not as much, but loved her just the same, and once when he came back home from school after she had moved out, that is, because Maria moved out of the house where her mother worked, one night after he came back he went to a dance, one of those town dances held in the public square, with much innocence, and she was dancing with a man, and David was drinking by himself in a corner until he got drunk, and then he suddenly went to where Maria was dancing and struck her partner with his fist and the man got up and started fighting with David, and Maria was astonished and then she put her hands over her face and she slowly began to cry, a cry of despair and hopelessness, that is, she cried so much that both men stopped fighting and looked at her, and David wanted so much to hold her in his arms and console her, but he didn't do it, and later he realized that by not doing it, he missed that rare chance, that once in a lifetime split moment chance given by God to all of us to make up for our mistakes, and when we miss that opportunity, then we spend a lifetime looking for another chance, but do not get it, and so David walked away, and it was left for Maria's dance partner to try to console her, but there was no consolation for her; and like I told you, David walked away, and the next day he did what was to become the pattern of his life: escaping- that is, he went away, back to the city where he was in school, but he failed, one failure after another, an endless procession of failures- in friendships, career, marriages- that is, failures multiplied by drinking too much, blaming too much, walking away too much; failures augmented by fears, cowardice, insecurities, escapes, and by this feeling that never left him, that he was living the wrong life, a feeling that weighed him down, a terrible weight, like the weight carried by sinners in hell, and it would have been so easy at one time to have lifted that weight, to fly in weightlessness, but he had chosen to carry the weight that slowly destroyed him, and a stronger man would have gone back, looked through his past with courage, identified where he had strayed and gone back when there was still time, but not David, a coward, a weak man, that is, a man like David could never have gone back; until one day a dream, a voice calling him from afar, and he, David, a broken man, without strength or will, a man whose dreams have left him like sea birds that leave a beach forever, for a hidden reason known only to them, never to return, but that time David did the only right thing he had done in his life- that is, he returned, and I still ask myself, what did he hope to find, was he so insolent to think that Maria and her, that is, his daughter would be waiting for him, and the truth is yes, he was hoping, because at that time he had not yet lost hope, but not so Maria or her child, who after years of unending work, and hunger, and shame, and despair, had been abandoned by that kindest of fairies, that is, by hope, and what are a lonely woman and a lonely child to do without hope; because you as a writer, a listening man, a story teller, you understand that everything can be lost, food, health, love, but not hope, because losing hope means losing everything, and Maria had lost all hope when her child, a quiet child like her, the sole remaining purpose of her existence, had died from a stray bullet, a destroyer of universes, a darkness seeker, shot by a soldier who had occupied the town, and a few days later they found Maria, lying beautiful and silent, as she had lived all her life, dead next to the river, and the people of the town said she had drowned while she was washing clothes; that is, they said that out of kindness, a kindness they had shown too late, and they told it to David, a cowardly man who understood, who understood the tremendous courage that it takes for a woman without hope to walk in tears into a river, talk to it, plead with it, and tell it of her suffering until it can be made to understand, and ask that its waters take her, and not fight back, and David, strangely, felt the same hopeless loneliness that she had felt in the river, and he, for the first time in his life, shed an ocean of tears, that is, true tears; and he had been right, because if he had come a few weeks before, and what is a few weeks, he would have found her waiting, like she had waited for him all his life, because there is a moment in time, a fraction of a second, a timeless moment, after which a mistake becomes uncorrectable, and more often than not we know exactly where that moment lies, and only if we had acted before that moment we could have changed everything, but too often, for hidden reasons, we allow that moment to pass by, and afterwards we would give so much to return, that is, to be placed once more before that moment, and David had missed that moment, and therefore he did the only thing he knew what to do; he left, as he had always done, always leaving what's most important, never to return, like those seabirds who never return. And from that point on he wandered from place to place, from cowardly act to cowardly act, trying to prove to the world and to himself that he could, at least once, be a courageous man, and disappointing the world, and more importantly, himself; and more than anything else he became a man in search of a woman to replace that woman, that without knowing, or knowing but not acknowledging, he had loved so much and would love forever, and Storyteller, what a hopeless search, because how can a loved one be replaced, an impossible task, as a man trying to dream the exact same dream that he had once dreamt; and that, my friend, is the end of my story, except that it hasn't ended, because the stories, like real life, continue forever; but it is only we who give them a false completion, perhaps because we need to rest; and what are you asking, if I am David in the story, but I told you before, that is, if you were listening, that I sometimes confuse what has happened with what I heard, or what I heard with what I saw, and dreams and reality become one, but at least I remember, not like the other people who have no memory, and they are always silent, as if they are atoning for a sin that happened long ago- so long that they have forgotten what it was, and now they only remember how to atone.

[Storyteller's note: Soon after finishing his tale, the old man got up and hurried out of the bar. Needless to say, his "stream of consciousness" story left me reeling. As I sat there listening to the old man's rambling, I had also been struck with another thought- was this the same old man who had told me of this town in the first place? I could not be sure, but "Lord," I thought, "what if it is?" And he had also said some strange

things about this town that made me wonder what kind of place it could be...Further reflection was cut short by the first person in the line, with an equally strange story to tell.]

 # The Soldier

[Storyteller's note: When compared to the old man, this fellow seemed normal enough- an "average citizen" one would say. But he had a strange look about him: peaceful and sad at the same time. I thought I had seen that look somewhere before...]

I guess my friend has finished his story, and from the look on his face when he left the bar, I imagine that what he's told you has caused him great distress. The bartender told me that he left in such haste that he didn't bother to pick up the money that you left him as payment. Shame, I imagine that he needs that money. In reality I do not know him well; I have only spoken to him once or twice, and even then we only exchanged a few words. But he seems to be a person who carries a great burden. You performed an act of kindness by listening to him.

It's now my turn to tell you my story. I was born in a fishing town on the eastern coast. My mother died when I was born; I was her only child. My father, his father

and his grandfather before him were all fishermen,
and it was also deemed by tradition that I continue the
trade. But I neither understood nor attempted to understand the way of the winds, the tides, or the migration
of fish.

A common love, like a common hate, can be the basis
for the strongest of bonds, and their love for the sea
created in my father and grandfather a relationship
between them that I admired and envied. They spent
much of the day together, and the sea was their most
frequent topic of conversation. They thought of the
ocean as a living being; they talked to it, pleaded with
it, and considered it at times the greatest of enemies,
and at other times the greatest of friends. The sea was
the life-giver and the life-taker, a capricious lord who
spoke and listened, if one used the right language.
They saw the waves as the beating of the sea's heart,
at times peaceful and soothing, at other times angry
and restless. And when I laughed at their beliefs, they
would argue; how could it be otherwise? How could a
man, weak and insignificant, venture out in the vastness
of the sea on a small boat powered by a small sail and
oars, unless that man could communicate with the sea
and ask it for shelter and mercy?

But in truth, the sea was more to my father than a
source of livelihood. He, like many of the fishermen,
was fascinated by the mystery possessed by the ocean:
the capriciousness of it, the changing of its colors

through the days and seasons, the sounds of its waves, the variability of its tides, and all of the other infinite phenomena displayed or possessed by the sea; some of which could be predicted and understood, but most of which was unpredictable and mystifying. And thus he was attracted to the ocean as a man is attracted to a mysterious woman, or a woman is drawn to a mysterious man, for no other reason than because he or she represents intrigue and enigma.

And when my grandfather grew old and could hardly manage the oars and the sails, he suddenly and without warning set out to sea one night. I remember that evening well. The moon was full and the sea was calm and peaceful. The moonlight reflecting on the water formed a white and clear trail that stretched from the beach to the horizon; and my grandfather, laughing and crying at the same time as though insane, rowed on the moon-trail furiously toward the point where the ocean and sky joined. He paid no heed to our cries from the beach asking him to return, and the few fishermen that set out after him in their boats could not catch up with him, so tenaciously did he row. That night was the last time that we ever saw him, and for years afterwards, when the fishermen talked about him, they spoke of that night almost with envy, as if they wished that they had the same courage my grandfather had, rowing out to sea when it came time for them to die. And, they argued, what better resting place than the sea for one who had spent more of his life on the water than on dry land.

My father was devastated by my grandfather's death. For years afterwards, on the nights when the moon was reflected on the ocean, he sat on the sand at the edge of the water and talked to his father as if he were there. I thought that he was going mad and frequently laughed at him until one night, and perhaps this was only a hallucination caused by the alcohol I had been drinking, I saw a dark figure sitting beside my father. When I approached, the figure got up from my father's side and walked into the moon trail on the water until it disappeared. And when my father looked at me that night without saying a word, I realized that despite being born there I was a stranger and an outsider to that village. The fishermen were simple people, content with their way of life, wishing little more than what they already had, and to my view, lacking in ambition.

But I was not like the other inhabitants of the village, and certainly not like my father or grandfather. Although I never admitted it to them, I was terribly afraid of the ocean, and it is difficult, although I know not impossible, to understand what one intensely fears. Because the mysteries of the sea held no fascination or wonder for me, the sea represented solely a source of livelihood. And thus I saw no reason to face my fears and continue a trade that had brought my family barely enough to survive, and during too many years not even that much. And so from an early age I began to look for a way out of the village.

SILENT SINNERS, SILENT SAINTS

Storyteller, I now realize as I look back on my life that I have spent far too much time attempting to get out of situations or circumstances. It is strange how much time a man devotes to this. It seems that life turns into a series of exits and entries, exiting a situation in order to enter another one, and vice versa. But I could not remain in the village.

What was there to do for a young man who owned nothing, without the ability even to read or write? I decided to take the only way out that was available to me: I became a soldier. My father objected. Between the members of my town and the army there had been for many years a high degree of animosity; legend and more than legend held that ours was a town of rebels, which in truth meant that we were a town of people who had fought for justice. But that had happened long ago, and I did not give the matter much thought. I left my village one morning and in two days reached the nearest army post. It was not hard for me to undergo the formalities required to join the army, and I quickly found myself in training camp. On the first day I was told that the army demanded two things: obedience and loyalty.

I have since learned, Storyteller, that neither obedience nor loyalty should be taken lightly. The object of obedience, the person or cause that we are obedient to, must be chosen with great care; that is, if we are able to choose, because frequently we have no choice in the matter. But if we do choose to be obedient to a specific person or cause, we are basically becoming the executioners of their will. We are kneeling before them holding our freedom on a tray, bowing our head and extending our arms and telling them, "Here I am, tell me what to do and I will do it." And how can a free man ever choose to do that, Storyteller? What real merit is there in absolute obedience, Storyteller, other than the forged sacred oath to it invented by those who exercise power? Because a free man who pledges unconditional obedience may never hope to remain free.

And now, after having been obedient for so long, I realize that self-imposed obedience is merely a shift of responsibility, a form of idleness that releases us from having to decide, a self-imposed cage that we walk into and close the door so that we do not need to go out wondering and exploring. I have been ruined by obedience, Storyteller, because earlier in my life I could use obedience as an excuse for what I did. But slowly, almost imperceptibly, one is overcome by the realization that a man is, in the end, responsible for his actions. Now I know that a true man, one who merits the name, does not shift upon someone or something else responsibility for his actions, because even by choosing obedience one is exercising choice and must be responsible for the consequences of that decision.

And in the same way, Storyteller, one must very carefully choose one's loyalties, because it is one of the most important decisions made by man. Loyalty is considered a great merit, but its only merit lies in the object of loyalty, and not in loyalty itself. As with obedience, it is a tool used by those who pursue power. Once power is achieved, the loyalty vanishes. Too often also, loyalty is the coward's only hope for achieving bravery.

Shortly after I joined the army a war broke out. On the day that we left the training camp to fight the enemy, an officer stood in front of us and explained who the participants of the battle we were about to fight were. We were told that we, the army and the government, were on one side, the humble fighters of a holy war, defending a holy cause. On the other side were the terrorists, communists, disturbers of the peace, destroyers of the country, enemies of the people, murderers of women and children. They were like cancer cells and needed to be utterly destroyed. And because by that time I had chosen to be obedient and loyal, I believed what they said. We, the soldiers, were excited- I more than most. From the son of a fisherman I had become the glorious defender of a country. We were told the enemy fought from the mountains, the villages, from caves; and we set out at once for this holy war.

But I should have understood then, like I understand now, that there is no such thing as a holy war. A benevolent God, as I have been taught God is, would not want human blood shed in His name. It only makes sense that if blood needs to be shed, He does not need humans to do it; there are ample options available to Him to achieve this task. So no holiness whatsoever is contained in war, or anything associated with it.

In the first few days of the war, I realized that something was not right. We encountered the enemy, but they weren't what I had envisioned. They were children, old people, all poorly armed, shuttering in the cold rain, some without shoes. Our officer was merciless in his administration of "justice". Torture was administered to women and children so that they would disclose the whereabouts of their husbands and sons. But I realized that the goal of the torture was not to obtain information, since the tortured person clearly did not know the answer to what was asked. Torture was applied because, in a way that I no longer understand, certain humans (if the term 'human' can still be applied to them) enjoy the suffering of others.

I often wondered how, on those days, when I could see the truth as clearly as I could see the tearful woman in front of me begging for me to acknowledge her, I chose not to believe that truth, and instead believed the lies told to us by our commanders. But, I asked myself, what did I, an illiterate fisherman's son, know of politics? If the government said that these people were the enemy, than who was I to disagree?

One day we started marching in the direction of my village. A terrible suspicion grabbed me. I prayed that we would turn off the road, go somewhere else, but deep in my heart I knew the truth. The name of my village had come up numerous times in the discussions between soldiers and officers. Not once did I speak up, never did I stand up to defend them before the others. And on this march toward my village I said nothing. For a fleeting moment I considered escaping the march, warning the village. But what I should have done, I didn't do.

When we arrived at the village, all of the men were gone. They had been forewarned of our coming, and all that was left were women and children. The officer was furious. He interrogated some of the old women, but nobody said anything. Then he gave an order. A lesson needed to be taught. The population was locked in the town church. I could see what was coming since I had seen it done before. And still I did nothing. The only grace provided me by God was that in the village nobody noticed me, and I did all I could to keep it so. That night the church was set on fire. Amazingly, only a few people screamed as they were burned to their death; the villagers were too proud to cry out. And once the church had caught fire, we left that village- my own village, my birthplace and that of my ancestors, and I have never returned because I do not deserve that privilege.

The moment in time in which a man's spiritual demise takes place can be as precise as the instant separating life from death. One can look back upon one's life, like looking at a movie, and clearly identify that moment. And frequently, one can foresee that moment seconds before it happens, and yet one does not prevent it from taking place. Why is that? Why miss that incredible opportunity to change one's history? I have pondered that question for many years and still don't know the answer. But in my case, that moment took place when I, after being ordered to do so, threw the first torch that burned the church.

I can see the look of horror and loathing in your eyes, but tell me: what could I have done? If I had said anything I would have been shot- considered a traitor. What would you have done? Tell me, what could I have done differently? It is too easy to condemn, because we do not know our potential, what we can be in extreme situations. Everything and everybody are made up of the most opposite of qualities: beauty and ugliness, weakness and strength, good and evil. It only takes the right set of circumstances to bring one or the other of these qualities to the fore.

After leaving my village we again began our march. We ended up in another village, where we were housed in certain homes for the night. One of the soldiers had stolen some liquor and I began drinking like I had never drunk before, perhaps to drown out the memory of the church. I walked out of the building, shouting, firing my gun wildly. And then it happened. One of the bullets struck a child. As in slow motion, I saw it all. The child, a little girl, fell without a sound, like a beautiful butterfly fluttering to the earth. Time stood still for an eternity; a silence such as I had never experienced had descended, almost like an invisible cloud, over the entire universe. Everywhere around there was silence, as if time had stopped in awe and respect for the dead child. For the rest of my life I will remember that silence; it was majestic, solemn and beautiful, and I was surprised to have caused it. And then the silence was broken by a horrible scream. A woman, perhaps the child's mother, ran toward the child, picked her up in her arms, and began rocking the dead girl. She was crying a cry the likes of which I have never heard before. It contained years of despair, resignation, and the deepest of loneliness and sadness. It was a cry signifying the loss of all hope- a cry for the child, for the woman, and strangely enough, for myself. I ran away, like a man assaulted by a spirit. For days I wandered aimlessly in the jungle. After days of sleeplessness, I was finally able to fall asleep. In the midst of that sleep I heard the most beautiful music that a man can hear. That music quieted my heart. I finally arrived at this place. I do not know how long I have been here, and I do not know how long I'll stay, but I suspect that I'll never leave.

It is strange how a man's life can change so quickly, and in the most unexpected of directions. From a fisherman's son I had become a hero, and from a hero, a murderer- all within a few weeks. And yet, I had only wished to escape being a fisherman for the rest of my life.

Daniel Drubach

The day I became a murderer was the day my life changed forever. I have become a different person. But what I remember most about that day was the moment of silence that followed the child's death. At the time I thought that it was the world sorrowing at the death of a child. Now I understand that it was meant for me. A kind God had stopped time, so as to give me a mirror in which to view the course of my life. I had murdered twice; I needed to stop. Without that moment I would have continued. I now realize that the circumstances in our lives take a certain course that carries us along, almost beyond our control. Our actions take a direction of their own and we follow them as machines, as prisoners, almost as if we weren't their cause. Moments of silence are needed to reflect, to stop, to re-plan our course. Moments of silence are indispensable as breaking points, to separate what was from what is to become. But by ourselves we lack the strength to create that silence, and instead we allow life to take us.

So this is the end of my story, a simple story. You seem to be appalled, but your horror could never outweigh my own, because personal horror, directed at oneself, is the worst of horrors. I hope that God was as kind to the mother of the child as He was to me.

[Storyteller's note: By the end of this story I had already begun asking myself, "Is this all real?" Remember, Dear Reader, where I am right now- or think I am. I am sitting in a little bar in a little town in Central

SILENT SINNERS, SILENT SAINTS

America! But the stories I am hearing are coming from people I would expect to find in heaven...or hell! "What kind of place is this," I asked myself, "where people simply line up and tell these kinds of stories? How much more of this can I take?" Well friend, just wait until you see who came next!]

The Man
With No Arms

[Storyteller's note: I had caught glimpses of him stand-ing behind "The Soldier," but I was paying such close attention to that man's story that I really did not get a good look at the fellow behind him. Well, when I did, I was amazed. He looked a mess. His face was full of scars, and his shirtsleeves hung loosely- I could see he had no arms!]

My name is Jorge Corral, but in this region I am known as "The Wanderer". I was born in a village on the other side of the country. My mother worked as a sugar cane cutter; I never knew my father. As you are aware, I'm not a particularly handsome man. My face and body are covered with scars. You are looking at me with an embarrassed look. It is true, I have no arms; I was born without them. When I was a child, the government doctor who came to the village once a month told my mother that it was due to some kind of birth defect. But my mother believed a different story. The summer that she was carrying me, and while she was cutting cane, a terrible tiredness overtook her, and she lay down to sleep in the middle of the field. She then had a strange dream. All of the trees and the animals had gathered in a circle, as though for a great congress. They were discussing one of my ancestors, a man legendary for his cruelty, who had killed many animals. I was to be born without arms so as not to become as he had been. My mother told me it was not a punishment, only prevention- an act of kindness to keep me from damnation.

My childhood was a painful one. The strong are forever oppressing the weak, and this strange aspect of human cruelty is even more evident in children. Unable to defend myself, I was always picked on by the other children. In a town where superstition is used to sate the ever-present hunger, a physical difference is seen as a personal fault, the punishment for some kind of hidden sin. The cruel thus justify their cruelty.

My mother, my only friend in the village, died when I was a child, and I grew up an orphan. At the age of eleven I embarked upon a journey which continues to date and perhaps will continue until the day of my death. When I left my village I owned nothing to take with me; just as well, having no arms with which to carry things, I could have taken no baggage. In fact, my inability to carry became one of the blessings in my life. In my travels I carry nothing, neither belongings, nor anger, worry nor sadness. People with arms believe that they must always carry. They tend to travel too heavily loaded, their passage through life made so much more difficult by their burden. So much of their strength is wasted in this carrying. Sometimes I wish they could be in my place if only for a few days, so they could realize that it is not necessary to carry so much. Anyway, what is most important one carries inside, and needs no arms to carry it.

A man without arms does not have hands with which to feel. He cannot touch a rock or a face. Instead, a man without hands learns to feel with his heart. And that is what I did on my journey. I slept in the middle of the forest, wherever tiredness overtook me. The wild animals did not harm me. They understood that a man with no arms presented them no danger.

I went from place to place with no set course. Shortly after I set out on my journey, I encountered a group of musicians playing music in the middle of the jungle. They didn't stop when they saw me and I sat down to listen. After they had finished their piece, a very old man came up to me and asked me to join them. "Without arms," I said, "I can play no instruments." The old man smiled sweetly. "Then you will become our singer," he answered. And that is how I discovered that I could sing. We traveled from place to place, playing our music, sometimes in cities and villages, but most of the time in the midst of the jungle. We usually had no audience save for the rivers, trees, and animals.

Once we encountered a woman who had lost all hope. She was crying by a river, and we understood that she had suffered a great loss- perhaps the death of a child. Without saying a word the leader of our band signaled us to set up our instruments. We played music for her for an entire day. Not a word was spoken, but when we left, she was at peace. On another occasion we found a sleeping soldier in the jungle. His sleep was troubled, as if he had committed a great crime. We played our music for him very softly. Although he didn't wake up, by the time we left, his sleep had become more peaceful.

We played our music to wounded animals that we encountered in the jungle, trees that were dying as a result of the logger's ax, river beds that lost their waters because of draught or dams, gusts of winds that were imprisoned in caves or children's balloons, children and adults that were suffering because of a gain or loss. We were never asked to play, and yet nothing and no one objected. We played and sang to relieve the pain, and we fulfilled a great need.

Once, as I was wandering by myself through the jungle, I saw a pillar of smoke in the distance. As I got closer I saw that it came from a burning church in a village square. I ran as fast as I could towards it. When I approached the church, it seemed as if the village was deserted. I cried out for help, but nobody answered. I circled the church and I saw a strange sight. The church door was nailed shut from outside. Then I understood. A war was going on in the country, and I had been told that the soldiers sometimes locked the population in the church and set it on fire. I never believed those stories because I could not envision human cruelty of such magnitude. But then I heard voices from within the church and I realized that those stories were true.

I despaired. Without arms I could not pry the door open. I finally ran into the door several times using my body as a catapult. The wood cut into my skin, but at the time I did not feel the pain, and the door finally gave in. Inside I saw a sight that I will never forget. Women and children were sitting on the pews, praying in loud voices, oblivious to the smoke and fire. They seemed to be in a collective trance. The people in the church had already accepted that they were going to die. I shouted, kicked some of them until they awakened from their state of sleep. I had to almost herd them out of the church. When all of them were out I went back into the church to make sure nobody else was inside, but a burning beam fell on top of me. I shouted for help, but the villagers were in too much shock to help me. With great effort I was able to crawl out by myself. And that explains the scars on my face and body.

The fire took away my ability to sing. For some time I wandered from town to town. Sometimes, the adults in those towns would call me to discipline disobedient children, or those needing to learn a lesson. These children were told that if they did not behave, I would be sent for, to take them away. But the plot almost never succeeded. Most children were not scared by me, despite my being a man with no arms and with a body full of scars. Most children in fact just smiled at me.

Loneliness has turned out to be the most loyal of companions. It walks with me during the day and curls up next to me at night. One wouldn't think so, but I search for it on the few occasions that it leaves my side. What is that you are asking me? If I am a happy man? That is an interesting question. I believe that grains of happiness are contained in moments all around us. They can be found in a piece of bread, a raindrop running down a leaf, a woman's smile, a change in the direction of the wind, an act of kindness performed by a merciful God. Those grains of happiness must be captured when first seen and used immediately, like manna falling from the sky that disappears if it's allowed to touch the ground. Grains of happiness cannot be stored and saved for the future. A man without arms realizes that he cannot pursue things that he cannot carry. Those grains of happiness are therefore his nourishment for living, his only and yet most beautiful of possessions.

You say that you admire my actions at the church? The world is full of compassionate sacrifices, if only one searches for them. Recently, as I was walking by a river, I saw what looked like a giant rock on the beach. A gigantic turtle lay overturned, helplessly lying on its shell. Its paws were moving in the air purposelessly, as if imploring heaven for an explanation for its suffering. She had probably emerged from the safety of the water to lay her eggs on the sand, and a fisherman had found her and overturned her. The fact that she was facing the water showed that her eggs had already been laid, hidden in the sand. The fisherman had probably left the overturned turtle there to get his tools, so that he would be able to butcher her. A turtle this size would provide enough meat to feed many hungry children.

As I approached, the turtle fixed her eyes on me. She looked at me with sadness and resignation, but without anger, recrimination, or fright. I thought of turning her over so that she could return to the water, but from the look she gave me I realized that it was too late. She was dying, making her last grasp for life; but her grief on leaving this world was eased by her understanding that her death was a sacrifice, one that was full of meaning. Her death would contain as much purpose as her life had held. With her eyes on me she made one final request. I understood, and with my feet I covered her tracks on the sand, so that the fisherman would not be able to find the eggs that she had buried. Then I sat next to her, and even though I had no singing voice since the fire, I sang to her as well as I could. I stood by her until she lay completely still, and I knew that she was dead. Then I continued on my trip until I arrived at this place.

That night I had a strange dream. All of the trees and the animals had gathered in a circle, as if for another great congress. I realized that I was being judged by them, on account of my ancestor. The turtle approached me and told me that on my account, my ancestor had been redeemed.

[Storyteller's note: The Man Without Arms turned and walked away as soon as he had concluded his story. The links that his story had formed between himself and the others before him were obviously unknown to him. I could not help but wonder why he had been un-able to hear them while he was standing there in line. But, I reasoned, those links must have been known to someone. I looked again at the bartender, but he kept himself busy at the end of the bar farthest from where I sat, and (purposely?) avoided looking my way.]

 # Manuel

[Storyteller's note: The next person in line to talk to me was a young man of about twenty-eight years. He looked average enough, but I knew that standing in line in this place he held many secrets.]

Mr. Storyteller, this is the story of Manuel. He was born in a small town not far from here. Manuel was different from the other boys in the village. Unlike them, he was gentle, almost delicate. It is because of this that the other children would refuse to play with him, and he grew up virtually alone. His father, a rough, hard working but ignorant man, never understood his son. In fact, he was embarrassed by Manuel's delicate manner, and even joined forces with the other men in the village in making fun of him. Manuel's mother was a kind but weak woman. She suffered from severe depression from the day of Manuel's birth, and did little in terms of her son's care. Manuel grew up practically as an orphan.

I met Manuel a few months after he arrived in the city. He had gone there as a young man in order to escape the most barbaric of human qualities: hate resulting from prejudice. In the city he became one lonely lost soul among many, but Manuel was well accustomed to those two feelings: loneliness and the sense of being lost. He found a job that paid him barely enough to survive, but for the first time in his life he was at peace- with the world at least, if not with himself. Manuel was followed everywhere he went by a strange yearning that he himself could not understand. His sweet smile, his gentle manner, hid a certain perplexity, a question for which he could find no answer.

And then one evening the understanding of his yearning came to him, like a gust of wind that suddenly, with no warning, picks you up and carries you, so that you, with no effort, become one with it. He was walking late at night in a deserted street when he came upon two people holding hands, whispering lovingly to each other in the shadows. They were startled when they saw Manuel, and tried to hide deeper in the darkness. But Manuel had seen what he needed to see.

It is strange how a person embarks upon a journey with a clear destination, one that stands directly ahead, always visible, so that the path is clear- like the Jews in the desert, with Mount Sinai in front of them, constantly indicating the way. But then, without warning, a different path with a different destination is shown to us- sometimes for such a fleeting moment that we are not even sure that it was more than an illusion.

But that fleeting vision changes everything. Even if we continue on the original path, we are unable to ignore that vision, because it has changed us if ever so slightly, but changed us just the same, so that we, the journeyers, are no longer the same people we were before. And that is what happened to Manuel when he saw those two people holding hands.

A swan grows up among flamingoes until it discovers it is a swan, and the yearning for its kind becomes a torment, the sole object of its life's quest. Manuel's yearning was that torment, a torment at last relieved by the end of his search.

When I met Manuel I immediately fell in love with him; gentleness is one of the most beautiful of qualities. Manuel was quiet gentleness. I, a person constantly caught in the path of cyclones, found peace by his side. But Manuel never allowed me truly close. When I attempted to approach him, his smile would gently, like a caress, push me away.

A person begins each day with the false certainty that by its end, nothing will have changed. But the course of our lives changes with so little warning. Once, as Manuel and I were walking in the port, we encountered a group of drunken soldiers. Cowardly men afraid of their own cowardice tolerate no threats to their hypocritical and false sense of braveness and manhood. The soldiers followed us, making drunkard threats, and ran up to us.

I ran away, but Manuel, a gentle giant, stayed behind and faced them. As I ran, I turned towards him. His face held a smile, a fearless smile. Why did he stay? Was he trying to protect me? Did he think he could fight that drunken group? Was he sacrificing himself for a hidden cause? I ran for hours, like a wild animal let loose in a city. The next day, I returned to the site of the attack. The street was deserted, but I went inside a shop and asked the shopkeeper about Manuel.

The greatest acts of kindness take place side by side with the greatest acts of cruelty, perhaps because one person's misfortune provides fertile ground for another's kindness. The shopkeeper told me that after the soldiers left, Manuel lay unconscious on the ground. A man with no arms and with his body covered by scars appeared out of nowhere. He screamed for help until other people arrived, and he never left Manuel's side.

When I arrived at the hospital where Manuel had been taken, I was directed to a large ward where the patients with no means were hospitalized. About a hundred men lay moaning in beds side by side, some with their eyes closed, others looking around the room with bewildered expressions. I went to a tired nurse and asked her for Manuel. She did not recognize the name, but after I described him, she suddenly said, "You mean the one accompanied by the man with no arms. He died yesterday, his body was taken to the school of medicine." Her voice was tired- it held no emotion. A silence ensued.

SILENT SINNERS, SILENT SAINTS

I asked for the man with no arms. "He left right after your friend died," she replied. I begged her to take me to Manuel's bed. It was occupied by a very old man with a long beard and closed eyes. I did not know what else to do and left the hospital. Once outside, I realized that it was a different world.

You ask me what brought me to this place. I have come in search of understanding. The motives for a person's actions are so frequently hidden from him. Perhaps one's greatest quest in life is to understand them. That quest supersedes all others, although at times it hides behind them. We dedicate so much of our lives to that quest, and we delude ourselves so often. We think we are searching for answers to so many questions, while in reality we are searching for the answer to one supreme inquiry: why is it that we do what we do? And thus I came to this forsaken place to attempt to comprehend. Why did I run when the soldiers attacked instead of staying next to Manuel? Why didn't I seek help? Why did I abandon Manuel when he most needed me? I loved Manuel, but he was never able to love me the way I loved him. Unrequited love is a cause for much sadness, but perhaps it is a cause for much more than that. I need to discover the truth.

But I am also here for yet another search. Meaning must be ascribed as much to a person's death as to his or her life. A meaningless death is as unfathomable as a mean-ingless life, and yet I still find no purpose in Manuel's death. But there has to be one, and I owe it to Manuel to find it.

[Storyteller's note: Having told his story the young man immediately walked off, as had the Man With No Arms. But wait! Had he not seen the Man With No Arms in this bar with him? It was he whom he had sought in his story, was it not? I turned to tell him that I had just seen the man he had been seeking, but he also was gone. He had disappeared into the haze. Yes, Dear Reader, a haze had crept into that barroom- a fog. Not only an auditory barrier, but now also a visual barrier separated, isolated, the souls standing in line. Indeed, by this time all I could see was the bar in front of me, the stool upon which I sat, and the next in the line of figures waiting to talk to me. I remember feeling almost like a priest in a confessional. But at the time I could not pause to think too much about it- as soon as the previous narrator departed, another quickly took his place.]

Amanda

[Storyteller's note: The next story was told to me by a big, burly fellow with an anxious look on his face, who literally burst in out of the haze. The people standing in line to talk to me looked impassively on as he pushed in out of nowhere to sit beside me. At the same time, I heard the bartender drop a glass, but I couldn't see him through the fog. Something "out of control," perhaps? I faithfully recorded what the big fellow told me, but I have to tell you, we were not in a café, and I had not been looking out the window at anyone! So, "where" had this guy been? To whom did he think he was telling his tale? At any rate, once he sat down he lost his troubled look and seemed to regain his composure, as if just sitting at the bar was therapeutic for him. I also relaxed. He seemed almost eager to tell me the following story.]

I noticed that you were looking at that young girl who just walked by the café. I feel I must tell you her story, which involves me in a certain way. Her name is Amanda. She was born in this town, a few blocks from where we are sitting. As an infant she did not seem to pay attention to those around her and she was thought to be "dumb" as they say, but a smart and observant villager realized that Amanda could not hear. Her parents, with good intentions, attempted to communicate with her through hand signs and gestures, but they became quickly frustrated and addressed her only occasionally. Amanda thus grew up in a lonely world, unable to communicate with those around her.

There was, strangely enough, another deaf child in the town, a frail boy of about the same age as Amanda whose name was Gabriel. Somebody thought they should meet, and from the time that they did, they were inseparable. They sat together in the small schoolhouse that all the children in the village attended, and because they found it difficult to communicate with their teachers or other children, they developed a language between them that nobody else seemed to understand. It consisted of gestures with their hands and faces, and even particular ways of looking at each other. At times they just looked at one another for hours at a time, with their faces still except for occasional smiles, as though involved in a silent and invisible conversation that required only their eyes.

They married very young, perhaps in their late teens. Both came from poor families, and the wedding itself was a small affair. Gabriel became the apprentice of a carpenter, and spent long hours in a dark carpentry shop. Amanda worked the fields, and every afternoon when she came back to her hut, she practically ran the entire way, so strong was her longing to see Gabriel. And so they lived, locked away in their own world, shunned by the other greater world of the village by their inability to communicate with the villagers, and apparently happy with their lot and with each other.

But one day, the soldiers came and took Gabriel away. The government was forcefully recruiting any man they could find to serve in their army, but I was exempted because my father was able to bribe a general. I am not sure what good Gabriel would have served them; he was small and frail, and as gentle as he was, I could not conceive of him as a soldier or a fighter. The soldiers took him away so suddenly that he did not even have time to say goodbye to Amanda. She was in the fields when they came for him, and when she returned to their hut and could not find him, she ran like a frightened bird to the government building to inquire about him. And on being made to understand that the soldiers had taken him, she dropped to her knees and wailed as if he were already dead.

People in the town commented that after Gabriel was taken away, the sole purpose of Amanda's existence became waiting for him. She continued to work in the fields, but every evening, when she could hardly walk because of tiredness, she would drag herself to the edge of town and sit at the side of the road, staring at the horizon in the direction that she had been shown he had been taken. And only when it was late night did she return to her hut.

A few days after his departure, a group of soldiers came into the village. Amanda approached them and through signs and gestures attempted to ask about Gabriel.
One of the soldiers told her, with no ceremony, that he had died from an explosion during one of the battles of the recent days. He had been buried on the side of the road, and only a cross with no name marked his grave.

I was sitting at the village canteen, a few feet away from the soldiers, when they broke the news of Gabriel's death to Amanda. I remember her face, her look of pain, just before she dropped, as though lifeless, on the ground. I picked Amanda up and carried her to her hut, and stayed with her until she regained consciousness.

It was loneliness and the terrible longing for Gabriel that drove Amanda into my arms. It was a need to mitigate a terrible sadness that could not be contained by any boundaries. I know that she held absolutely no love for me, and that my arms could have been the arms of any other man that happened to be there at that precise time. And I stayed with her that night, not because I had any sympathy for her, but because I was a selfish brute who saw no fault in sleeping with a lonely woman whose pain was so intense that she did not know what she was doing.

SILENT SINNERS, SILENT SAINTS

But Gabriel had not died as the soldiers had reported. The day after he was reported dead, a lonely, limping figure walking as fast as he could was seen approaching the village at dusk. The farmer who on the way to the fields met with Gabriel later told me that he did not initially recognize him. Gabriel had long unkempt hair and had thinned out even more than he already was when he left the village.

And when Gabriel suddenly and with no warning entered the hut, a broad smile on his face, he found me half-dressed, standing by the bed. Amanda was sleeping and did not see Gabriel enter. What happened next continues to haunt me, and the events return to me almost nightly as a recurrent nightmare that keeps me from being able to sleep in peace. I can clearly recall Gabriel's face, changing from a smile to a look of sadness, and then to frank rage, right before he attacked me. I tried numerous times to exit the hut, but Gabriel kept charging me, rage perhaps blinding him to the point that he could not see that his charges had little effect on me. I was much stronger and heavier, and I only needed to stretch my arms out to keep him away from me, as if he were a child. By this time Amanda had awakened and looked confusedly at first, and later with a look of horror, at both of us. She sat immobile, as if paralyzed by her disbelief.

On one occasion when Gabriel charged me with increased intensity, I quickly moved to the side and he came past me, his head striking a heavy iron rod that was used to stir the fire in the wood stove. He seemed to pause for a moment, looked back at Amanda with what I think was a look of profound tenderness and good-bye, and then at me with a look of rage. He then dropped to the floor, and so still was he lying on the ground, I knew immediately that he was dead.

I only have vague recollections of what happened next, but I do remember that Amanda knelt next to Gabriel's body and let out a terrible wail, the likes of which I have never heard before. I left the hut and went to my own home, and only the next day did I go to the police station and report to them what had happened. When the police arrived at Gabriel's hut they found Amanda still kneeling by Gabriel's body, her head on his chest, as if they were both sleeping. She did not resist when they gently pushed her aside and took his body to the morgue. He was buried the next day, the funeral procession comprised only of Amanda and the priest, and of myself from afar. And every day from then on, when Amanda returned from the fields, she sat next to his grave and talked to him in their own secret language, with gestures of the hands and face, and with long and silent stares.

I often wonder whether I had any blame in Gabriel's death. After all, both Amanda and I believed him dead, and she, if not I, would not have done what she did if she thought him alive. But somehow this does not serve as a consolation; to me Amanda was just a woman I could find satisfaction with for one night; to Gabriel, she was his life, and I am terribly saddened by the hurt that I so selfishly caused both of them. However, I am comforted by one belief that I desperately hope to be true. From the look on Gabriel's face when he attacked me that night, I gather that he believed that I was there against Amanda's will, that it was I who had come to the hut to rape her and found her sleeping, and that Amanda was not at all to blame. And this explains his look of tenderness and good-bye, with no trace of anger, when he looked at Amanda before he died. And I hope that this assumption is correct, because it would have been adding so much pain to pain if he had believed otherwise.

[Storyteller's note: After hearing this story I came to realize that I was serving as a reporter for people whose stories had to be told somehow. So often they spoke of dreams, of guilt. Was I put there to serve as some sort of relief for them? Had I truly become a confessor figure? The bartender, when I could see him at all, continued to seemingly ignore me, offering me no help or explanation. I came to the conclusion that these people, these souls, were undergoing some sort of spiritual encounter here, and that I served merely as the conduit, the vehicle, for that encounter. So I decided to sit there and do my duty!]

The Shared Dream

[Storyteller's note: The next person to approach me was well dressed and appeared average in every way. I felt relieved to see such a person in this strange place!]

The story I am about to tell you began with a strange, recurring dream. I am not entirely confident that my recollection of the dream is accurate, since so many months have elapsed since I last dreamt it. I have also discovered that on each subsequent retelling of the dream I seem to add a new detail- the color of an object, or the direction of the wind- and I am not sure whether this is due to a new memory which for some reason lay previously dormant, or to the workings of my imagination striving to fill the blanks and omissions that are so frequent in dreams.

There is nothing particularly notable about the dream itself. The setting was that of a flat desert surrounded by what appeared to be high mountains, some of which occasionally expelled fire and smoke from their tops. I presume that these were erupting volcanoes. It was twilight, and the sky shone with a soft, red glow. I rode a tall black horse. Two other riders rode behind me in single file. All three of us wore long, white tunics that covered our entire bodies, including our shoes. The other two riders' faces were covered by white cloths as worn by Bedouins in the desert, and only their eyes could be seen. There was absolute silence, and no sound came from the volcanoes as they periodically erupted. The horses walked with some difficulty as their hooves dug into the soft sand. This was the entire extent of the dream, nothing else happened in it. There was no great plot. But it recurred almost nightly for several nights. And so, out of curiosity, I decided to decipher its meaning.

In a town near my own there lived a dream interpreter of some renown. He was an old man, so old that not even the oldest inhabitants of the town had any memory of him ever having been young. His face was so wrinkled that its features could no longer be discerned. As a child he had been trained in the secret rituals of dream interpretation by the natives of the northern jungle, and since few of them had survived the multiple tribulations caused by the frequent wars in the area, the old man was perhaps the sole remaining practitioner of this ancient art.

People from the region came to the interpreter not only for him to decipher their dreams, but also to modify their content, for it was rumored that he could enter a recurrent dream as an actor enters the stage of a play in progress. Once inside the dream he could pick up an object and remove it from the dream, or light a candle in a dark room so that the dreamer could better see what it contained. He was even able to persuade characters in the dream to leave or to change their actions. He accomplished his work by prescribing a concoction of sorts that induced in the client a deep sleep, a necessary condition for the interpreter to perform his job. And upon awakening, the dreamer frequently recalled being a witness to the interpreter at work.

For these curious services he charged variable fees, at times quite high. He justified his rates by claiming that entering and modifying a dream was not only difficult and exhaustive, but in fact could also be extremely dangerous. It was possible, for example, that an unwelcome character in a dream could not be persuaded to leave, and then it became necessary to remove him by force. This, he argued, was not an easy feat, especially since with advancing age his strength had begun to fail him. He also remembered that on one occasion a terrible storm had begun suddenly within a client's dream; the river had risen and he had almost drowned in the flood that followed. But he had learned his lesson. Since he had never been a strong swimmer, he now knew better than to enter dreams that contained deep water.

When I recounted my dream to the interpreter, he listened attentively, holding his hands over his eyes so that nothing would distract him. But when I finished my account, he suddenly opened his eyes and appeared to be quite excited. He told me that on the previous day, a person who lived in a town a few miles away had told him the exact same dream. The interpreter could only identify one difference between the two. In my dream I was the person riding the first horse, while in his he rode the second. In each of our dreams we could identify ourselves, but not the other two riders.

I was stunned by the interpreter's comments and immediately set out to find the other dreamer. He turned out to be a red headed man of about my same age, a pharmacist by trade. When I related to him my experience with the interpreter he seemed extremely surprised. I don't think that he thought it possible for two individuals to have the same recurrent dream. And so we decided to tell each other our dreams. We debated as to who would relate his dream first, fearing that it would influence the other person's account. It was the pharmacist who came up with the obvious solution. Each of us would simultaneously write our dream on a piece of paper and after we were done, hand it to the other person.

I still remember the look of surprise that he displayed, and I suppose I also did, when he read the paper that I handed him. As to myself, I could not contain my excitement. His dream was exactly the same as mine, including the color of the riders' clothing, the number of volcanoes, and the feelings that the dream elicited in each of us. Everything else coincided except that, as the interpreter had said, we were aware of ourselves in the dream and thought of the others as strangers. Also, while I was riding the first horse in the line in my dream, he was riding the second in his. And in each of our dreams, it was our own face that was uncovered, while the other two riders wore a scarf that only revealed their eyes.

We spent quite some time discussing the significance of two people having the same recurrent dream on exactly the same nights. And it suddenly dawned on us that there was a third person in the dream who probably was also an inhabitant of the non-dream reality and had also dreamt the same dream. We debated as to the identity of that individual. My co-dreamer believed that it was a woman, but I argued that it was a man. Neither of us could clearly delineate the reason for his belief; I thought that the third person's eyes and stare were harsh and manlike, but my co-dreamer felt that the look was gentle and soft. He also had noticed the third person's hands, which appeared to be soft and small like those of a young girl. I admitted that I had paid no attention to this detail and could neither support nor contradict his observation.

As our conversation progressed, we kept coming back to our intrigue with the identity of the third person. We realized that any clues that could potentially clarify the issue would necessarily be contained within the dream itself, and we decided to search there. Since we expected the dream to recur, we agreed to try to discover as much as possible about the third person while we were dreaming and discuss it with each other on the following day.

That night, similar to what had been occurring for weeks now, I had the same dream. Again I found myself riding the tall dark horse. But this time I turned my head back to gaze at those behind me. And in the seemingly lightening moment before I awakened, I noticed three things: the reddish curls that were visible emerging from the second rider's head scarf, and the delicate feminine-shaped hands and beautiful dark piercing eyes of the third rider. In his own dream that night, the pharmacist had also noticed the hands and eyes of the third rider, but when he tried to turn his horse and ride alongside, he was unable to turn the reins. It was as if his hands were paralyzed and could do no more before he awakened.

We realized that it was difficult for a dreamer within a dream to follow through with a task that he had planned during wakefulness. We thus decided to enlist the services of the dream interpreter. We found the old man sitting in his hut looking at the back wall, and he did not turn to us when we spoke. But after listening to our request, he suddenly turned towards us with a piercing look. It could be dangerous, he argued, and we needed to understand the danger. We replied that we would pay him his usual fee, and so make it worthwhile for him to endure the risks. But with an almost compassionate voice he replied that it was not he who would endure the danger; it would actually be the two of us.

I must admit that at the time I thought his remarks almost comical, and perhaps even cunning. I thought that he was purposefully adding mystery to mystery so as to incite us to pay a higher fee. But when I laughed and looked at him, I realized that he was sincere. And it was precisely the sense of potential danger that added fuel to our curiosity and made our resolve even stronger. Finally, upon our insistence, the dream interpreter agreed. He instructed us to taste no food or drink for at least eight hours prior to going to sleep, and when we felt that sleep was imminent, we were to drink a concoction made from a fistful of herbs that he gave to each of us.

That night I had difficulty falling asleep, which for someone who only needs to rest his head on a pillow to be struck with immediate sleep, is quite an unusual occurrence. I tossed and turned in bed for several hours before falling into a light and restless slumber. But when the dream finally came to me, it lacked the clarity of other times. Everything appeared visible as if through a cloud of smoke. Images became distorted and faded, like wet paint sliding down a freshly painted canvas. And then, from the edge of the dream, apparently at a great distance, I vaguely distinguished a person walking with a slow and unsteady gait in the direction of the horsemen. It was the dream interpreter who, ignoring the second horseman and myself altogether, approached the third rider. I could not discern the dialogue between them, but the last thing I remember before I awakened was that the third rider dismounted, sat on the ground next to the old man, and uncovered her face. And I saw, very clearly now that the haze had suddenly dissipated, that it was the face of a beautiful young woman, perhaps the most beautiful woman I had ever seen.

As we walked together to the interpreter's house the following day, the pharmacist related the dream he had had the previous night. It had been exactly as mine. The pharmacist appeared quite excited; he had been struck by the woman's beauty and had not been able to stop thinking about her since he had awakened. And then he asked me, was it possible to fall in love with someone in a dream?

We discussed this question at some length. There were obvious risks to having a dream lover. What was one to do with one's feelings of love during wakefulness since the object of that love was only present during a dream? And what if the dream were not to recur; what would one do with that love then? There was, we concluded, too much potential sadness in such a situation. But it is also true, we agreed, that there are indeed many who go through life in love with an object that is only present in their dreams.

SILENT SINNERS, SILENT SAINTS

When we next met with the dream interpreter, he spoke to us in a much kinder tone than he had in the past. He assured us that he had entered our dream and talked to the third person at some length. It was indeed, as we already knew, a beautiful young woman. Her life had been one of recurring sadness. When barely more than a child she had been abducted from her village by a gang of rebels from the north. During her abduction she had suffered unspeakable horrors, but managed to escape with the help of one of the rebels. She later gave birth to a child, and in order to feed him was forced into prostitution. But despite it all, the interpreter said, she continued to be a beautiful human being- an angel fallen from grace who, despite the fall, had remained a beautiful angel.

Both the pharmacist and myself were moved by the dream interpreter's account. The pharmacist especially kept probing the interpreter for more information about the woman, but he could tell us nothing more. And as we left the interpreter's hut, the pharmacist broke into tears. He confided that he had fallen in love with the woman and, he asked, if he were unable to find her, what would he do with that love? But I did not know how to answer, and so said nothing. For the next several weeks I did not dream. Every night I would go to sleep hoping that the dream would recur. I had a longing, if that is what it could be called, to see the woman again. But I awakened disappointed, and frequently sad and ir-ritable as well.

Finally one night I dreamt again. The setting was the same as the original dream, the same desert, with the mountains and erupting volcanoes in the distance. It was also twilight, but in contrast to the other dreams, all three of us had dismounted and our faces were uncovered. The three horses stood together at some distance. The pharmacist and myself were involved in a struggle. We moved in a circle, facing each other, each of us holding a dagger in our right hand. The woman was silently sitting on the ground a few yards away. Her eyes were fixed on us with a blank expression. Periodically the pharmacist and myself would lunge at each other. I remember the pharmacist's red curls covering the front of his forehead, and he made frequent quick movements of his head to remove them from his vision. Except for our occasional panting, it was absolutely quiet. And then the pharmacist lunged at me with particular force but lost his footing. He dropped to the ground and I stabbed him in the chest. He made a few sounds, as though he could not breath, and finally stopped moving. I dropped the dagger. The woman got up and began walking toward me. When she got near, she smiled and took my hand. And then I awakened.

I could not return to sleep. When light was barely visible on the horizon I walked as fast as I could toward the pharmacist's home. Several times I knocked on his door but there was no answer. Then a neighbor emerged from the adjoining house and informed me that the pharmacist had died during the night. Before his death, the neighbor had heard choking sounds. When he went to investigate, a large red bruise could be seen on the dead pharmacist's chest.

And I must confess that since that day I have been searching for that woman. She has abandoned my dreams altogether, although very occasionally I seem to return to the desert. But in those dreams I walk alone, and I suppose that I am looking for her. So I search for her in both worlds, that of dreams and that of wakefulness. That is how I arrived at this town. And that, Storyteller, is the essence of my story.

[Storyteller's note: "Could such a story be true?" I asked myself. The fervor with which it was told proved to me that the teller certainly believed it to be. I meant to ask him a myriad of questions, but like the others, he quickly vanished after he had related his tale. I wondered how he had known of this town, or had he? He had "arrived" here, but was it voluntary? Was he dreaming now? Were we all dreaming? The next person to sit down let me know just how "personal" this experience was for me.]

The Palm Reader

[Storyteller's note: Next came an old woman- the first of the two "gifts" I received that day.]

The people here have been telling you their stories. I, instead, will reveal your own story to you. Do not be afraid of my appearance, Mr. Storyteller. It is true, I am an old woman, wrinkled and unkempt, and people here think I'm an old witch. But glance beyond my looks, Storyteller. I have been given a special gift: to see people's lives, past and present, secret and revealed, by looking at the palms of their hands. I can reveal to people things about themselves that they themselves don't know, because most people possess very little self-knowledge.

Do not be afraid to give me your hands. You have come here searching for something; but you, like most, do not know the object of your search. Searching for an unknown object is not a search at all, Storyteller; it is merely being lost. Let me reveal that object to you. But you must have courage; you store far too much fear inside. And living in fear is no life at all. One must live with extreme caution, but fear must be put aside.

Give me your hands, Storyteller; I will be careful. I will tell you your past, but your future will remain my secret. I know too well that humans are barred from seeing their future as an act of kindness. Such knowledge would make them slaves of their own destiny. But humans hide too much from themselves, Storyteller, and by doing so they fail to live fully. So do not be afraid to hear that which I have to tell you.

Your hands are soft, much like your heart, which is crying, like a woman who has lost all hope. Let me relieve that pain, Storyteller. Let me take it from you, because I, I have become accustomed to pain. I know what it is that ails you. It is a craving for a certain knowledge: your roots. Roots are as important to a man as they are to a tree; lacking them, a person goes through life swaying from side to side. With nothing holding him to the ground, he lies at the mercy of the winds of the present and future. On the day that you were separated from your roots, you were a young child. It happened so long ago that you do not remember it well, but in the deepest recesses of your mind the vestiges of that memory remain, like a wounded animal that hides in a cave, resigned to die, but death refuses to come.

Your father was a shoemaker. He went from town to town, from door to door, selling his shoes. He was a rough man; everything about him was rugged. His enormous hands were as rough as the crude leather he worked with to make his shoes. He seldom spoke, he wore silence as one who wears a cloak, and there were many who had never seen him smile.

One day he knocked upon the door of your mother's house. She was only a child at the time, no more than fifteen. Upon looking at the shoes that your father was offering for sale, she burst out laughing. Mockingly, she told him that she would never be caught wearing those shoes. Your father looked at her for a long time without speaking, but before she closed the door on him he swore to her that one day she would indeed wear them. She laughed again, but the encounter had both frightened her and aroused her curiosity. However, she told no one about it.

A few days later your father abducted your mother as she was walking to a pharmacy. Locked in his enormous arms, she was unable to scream or wrestle herself free. He took her to an abandoned house at the outskirts of the town. The whole town searched for her the entire night with no success. The next morning, she was found walking silently in the streets of the town.

Except for your mother and father, no one knew what happened the night they spent together in the abandoned house. The next morning, back in her own house, your mother refused to answer any questions. The people in the town apprehended the shoemaker, who offered them no resistance, but like your mother, he refused to give any information. After a few days of constant questioning he was released and left the town.

Your mother's life changed completely from that day. From being a talkative, blissful child she became a quiet woman. She refused to relate what happened that night, and rumors started circulating in the town that she had willingly spent the night with the shoemaker. The people whispered about her when she walked by; women made the sign of the cross and crossed to the other side when they encountered her in the street. But she said nothing, despite constant questions by her parents and even the priest, who upon her silence also began believing the rumors.

One day she disappeared from the town, never to return. A few weeks later rumors reached the town that she had been sighted walking in the desert behind the shoemaker, both of them carrying bags full of shoes. Her family, disgraced by her behavior, held a funeral for her as though she had died. From then on they were seen throughout the country, he always walking in front and she a few feet behind. No one ever saw them talking to one another. He continued to go into towns selling his shoes from door to door, but she always stayed on the outskirts.

From this strange union twelve children were born. Only four were able to survive the constant marches from town to town. You were the last to be born. When you were three years old, a civil war broke out in the country. The desert was plagued by bands of scoundrels who took advantage of the disorder in the country, and one of those bands found your family walking in the desert. Your father fought bravely, desperately attempting to defend his family, but both he and your mother were cruelly slaughtered. You and your brothers were left to die in the desert, but a patrol of soldiers found you and took you to an orphanage. Your siblings were separated, never to see each other again. You were never told where you came from.

One detail of the story merits clarification. Your father did not rape your mother that first night. He took her to the cabin and then set her free. She elected to stay the whole night, staring at him sleep from a corner of the room. That whole night they did not exchange a word. In the morning she got up and left; he made no attempts to retain her.

Storyteller, awaken from the sleep that has kept you in its midst for so many years. A person ignorant of his past is a prisoner of the present and of the future, a slave to dreams and illusions. You deserve to be free.

[Storyteller's note: So I "slept." Ah! I felt a release with her words, and came to realize just how powerful words could be. I saw also that those telling me their stories were perhaps not the only ones who benefitted from that telling.]

The Pendulum Man

[Storyteller's note: Next came a slender, agitated man. He spoke very rapidly, swinging from side to side as he did so. I received from him more a stream of consciousness than a story, and I perceived that he represented much more than a solitary man. He was, rather, a living allegory. And my new awareness (imparted to me somehow by the palm reader) also told me that his only reality was there in that barroom.]

Mr. Storyteller, I am a swift man. I move, from side to side, like a pendulum, from one extreme, to the other extreme, always moving, never still. I lean, from right to left, from left to right, from day to night, from sleep to wakefulness, like a sea wave, that comes in, and then goes back, and I constantly sway, from dreams to reality, then back into dreams. And one moment I'm awake, and the next moment, I'm asleep, and in a dream, and sometimes I can't tell, which is reality, and which the dream, and sometimes, they are both the same. And some people tell me, it's a disease, they think I'm crazy, to move so much, from being awake,

to being asleep, but I can never stay still. And it is not
an ailment, but a special gift, that allows me to see,
always both sides, of anything. I see a man alive, and
in a few minutes, in a dream, I see him dead, and later,
alive again, and I see the sinner, and the saint, in the
same man, because in every man, there is a secret sinner, and a secret saint, and a man may be happy, but
then I see, in a dream, or in reality, sometimes I can't
tell which, a sickness, that will overtake him, and I cannot tell him, because he would never believe, so I keep
it all inside, this special power, of seeing both sides,
to everybody and everything, and there is always, two
sides, and never one, and thus I sway, from right to left,
from left to right, and from the right I see one thing,
and then, I run to the left, as fast as I can, and from
there, I see something else, so different, from the right,
and a man goes to sleep, while it's raining, a terrible
storm, and while he sleeps, the rains stops, and the
sun comes out, a bright, warm sun, a precious day, and
the birds sing, and the ground becomes dry, but then, a
cloud comes, from afar, and covers the sun, and it starts
raining, and wets the ground, and the birds hide, and
the man awakens, and sees the rain, a terrible storm,
and he thinks, that while he slept, it rained, all through
his sleep, and so many men, go through so much, of life,
asleep, missing so much, because so much happens,
while we are asleep, so much, we cannot see; but I see
the spaces, between rain and rain, and sun and sun,
nothing escapes me, like that soldier, an old man now,
but when young, he killed a child, he burned a church,

a great sinner, a killer, but that is only, when one looks,
from the left side, because if I run over, as fast as I can,
to the other side, I see an afternoon, many years ago,
in a desert, with a scorching sun, a shoemaker, with his
wife and children, a tired man, a decent man, and a
band of scoundrels, men with no conscience, no soul,
no understanding, that when you kill a man, you destroy, an endless score, of generations, his children, and
grandchildren, not yet born, an entire universe, an endless chain, and when you kill one man, or one woman,
you interrupt that flow, you change the universe, and
those scoundrels, attacked the shoemaker, and the soldier, running aimlessly, escaping from himself, saw it
from far away, and like a wild animal, a man possessed
by demons, he ran, a single man, armed with courage,
and pity, and a knife, against twenty killers, and he attacked the scoundrels, without fear, and the bandits,
surprised, angered, wounded by a knife more ferocious
than the hand that held it, could not kill this soldier,
one possessed, and wounding him they left, supposing
him a demon, with the shape of a soldier, leaving the
shoemaker and his wife dead, but sparing the children,
not because of pity, but because of the soldier, who
made them forget, long enough, to save them, the children, and thus you see, a killer of universes, of generations, and at the same time, a savior of universes, of
endless generations, that were brought to life, much
later, by those frightened children, who were saved, by
a soldier, who still today, seeks atonement, perhaps already, pardoned by God, but never able, to pardon him-

self. But I, a swift man, who moves, from side to side, like a pendulum, from one extreme, to the other extreme, always moving, never still, I can see both sides, the sinner, and the saint, in the same man.

[Storyteller's note: I knew the Pendulum Man would not simply walk away, but rather would vanish. And so he did. I also realized for the first time what the soldier meant to me!]

Rust to Gold

[Storyteller's note: Later, after all of this was over, I realized that what had gone before in this strange place had only been a preparation for this last interview and the two stories that the bartender was to tell me afterward. This woman (who did not at all look old, despite what she said of herself) had an almost angelic appearance, and seemed to radiate an aura of goodness. In my newly "awakened" state I had no trouble observing that aura. At the end of her very long story, which (it seemed obvious to me) contained as many symbolic experiences as it did "real" ones, I realized that she, like the palm reader, had been sent to me for a very special reason. She was the second "gift" imparted to me by...whom?]

My story is one that has occurred multiple times, and will continue to repeat itself until mankind is no more. Thus, there is nothing novel about the story that I will tell you. While the individual circumstances may vary, you have heard it many times in the past and will hear it multiple times in the future because the essence of my story lies rooted in the very nature of man.

I need not point out to you that I am a prostitute. I am only 38 and yet I am extremely old, partly because I am so weary, and partly as a result of the experiences I have been through. Age is not determined only by the passage of time, but also by the experiences one accumulates throughout one's lifetime. And my experiences have aged me greatly.

The course of my life may be compared to someone who crosses a river by stepping on stones barely visible in the water. One can never be sure that such a stone will provide support until one is actually standing upon it. And even then, no matter how strong one's initial footing seems to be, it happens too frequently that the stone begins to move and one is in danger of falling into the current. So quickly, without pausing to think too much about it, one must jump onto another stone, once more hoping that it will hold. And then one finally realizes that no matter how steady it may seem when one initially steps on it, the stone will always move, because it is our own weight, the weight resulting from our history, that causes it to shift. And so one must constantly be prepared to jump again and can never take the time to fully rest, because that rest may lead to destruction. Because I am on that river I realize that eventually, sooner or later, I will fall. Fear is the main cause of hesitation and falling; and Storyteller, it is becoming very difficult for me to keep myself from being afraid.

So now I jump, each time with less vigor, from hope to sadness, sadness to hope. But there was a time, not too

distant in years but infinitely far in events, when that
was not so. I was a child, innocent, cheerful, and if it
can be believed (I say with a pride that almost makes
me laugh at its ridiculousness) not particularly bad looking. But at the time being pretty and young was not a
blessing, but rather a curse. There was, as there always
was and will always continue to be, a war going on.
And you know, Storyteller, that since the beginning of
mankind there has been a continuous war, never ending
even for a brief moment; only the place and the ones
fighting change, as if each village, each culture, each
country takes a turn and then gives the turn to somebody else, so as to have a temporary break, a moment
of peace. But man quickly tires of peace, and a few
years or generations later that same group of people
takes back their turn and renews their fighting. There
is no need for a particular reason or cause. Man makes
himself believe that there is a motive, a justification for
the war. But the reasons that man invents for the war
are fictitious; they are invented to justify the need to
fight. And it is sad to say, Mr. Storyteller, that the reasons for war are not the ones given, but the ones obvious: an excuse to plunder, rape, loot, and destroy. And
those who do not do the actual fighting live the fighting
through the fighting of others, which explains why man
is so fascinated with war. War is the subject of so many
stories and books. It seems that without war, there is
not sufficient excitement in man's life.

And the saddest victims, the ones who most often have
nothing to do in starting the wars, are the ones who

most suffer: the women and children, those most likely to be defenseless and powerless. The ones that have the least need for war are the ones most likely to be consumed by it. And thus my story, Storyteller. My fall from grace began about ten years ago. I remember the exact moment, the feeling of horror that possessed me when a sound like thunder broke the silence of the night that we falsely believed covered us, my parents, brother and myself, with peace and shelter. A hundred men, or perhaps a thousand, came shouting and shooting weapons into our village. They kicked the doors open to every house and forced all of us- men, women and children- to line up in the street.

What followed is too horrible and too painful to recount. The attackers, for no reason at all, began to shoot people at random in the line. I saw my adopted mother, the person I loved most in the universe, fall with blood coming out of the side of her head. And I will never forget the look of horror, of wonder, of question, in my little brother as he fell next to her, as if asking for the reason for this senselessness. And then, without giving us time to realize what had happened, the attackers left, taking us, the young girls, the prettiest of us, with them.

I will not tell you the horrors that we endured afterwards, but I will tell you that I died that night. You sound surprised by my words, but it is not necessary for one's heart to stop beating for one to die. One dies upon realizing that the life lived until then is forever lost, never to be recovered, because everything that we had, everything that we were, our very essence, was taken away. And as one settles in the new life and remembers the prior one, one cannot help but wonder whether it had been real or merely an illusion, a dream. I remember that it was a difficult death, because I did not want to leave that previous life behind. And so I mourned for a long time, only to realize that I needed to stop the mourning if I had any hope of being born again.

But even in the darkest of horrors there can be found a small measure of light because the brightness of a candle can only be truly appreciated and understood relative to the light or darkness that surrounds it, and the smallest candle in the darkness of the night can appear much brighter than the largest and brightest candle in the sunlight. And amidst the darkness of my captors there was a man named Malus who seemed to timidly and secretly irradiate some goodness. Although he was a member of the group of savages that committed horrible atrocities on a daily basis, he seemed to do so reluctantly, almost as though he were forced. Compared to the rest he was less brutal, at times almost compassionate. Frequently, when others were not watching, he would bring us prisoners water or food, and on a few occasions quietly provided us with words of encouragement. He told us he had overheard that the war was close to ending, that our captors would disband, and that we would soon be free.

He was especially kind to me and I realized that he had taken a liking to me. At first I was terrified and avoided his attention, but in a few days I welcomed the fruits that he would secretly bring me, the almost bashful smile that he directed at me. My fellow prisoners also welcomed this attention towards me and we decided to use it to our advantage in an attempt to escape.

And one night, at his insistence, I lay with him. I did so because I knew that if I did not consent I would be forced, and I needed him on our side in order to escape. In other words, Mr. Storyteller, I was using him as much as he was using me, or perhaps I was using him more, because while he seemed to hold a genuine degree of affection towards me, I held nothing for him except hate and fear. I remember that night clearly because I had a curious experience that I will never forget. As I lay with him, I seemed to rise above myself and look at us lying there, as if I was an outsider. And almost with a sense of wonder and curiosity I looked at the individual that I had become and realized how different I was compared to only a few weeks before, when I had been just a child. And I realized that never in my wildest imagination would I have considered doing then what I was doing now. It occurred to me how little we know ourselves, or of what we are capable of doing, or of becoming. And as I looked at myself lying there I thought that perhaps I was dreaming, but I was not sure which was the dream, the life I had now, or the life I had previously lived.

SILENT SINNERS, SILENT SAINTS

During the nights that I was with him, Malus told me much about his life. I believed he did so because he had the need to justify to both himself and to me the reasons for his present behavior. He was from a town close to the ocean and he frequently expressed a longing to return. He frequently spoke of a woman whom he had loved dearly, but who had taken her own life by drowning in a river. I could tell from the silence that followed when he talked about this woman that he felt somehow responsible for her death. I could also detect a great deal of sadness when he talked about her, and once he confessed that from the first time that he had seen me I had reminded him of that woman. And I often wondered whether this memory was the sole reason for his affection toward me. Malus also told me with tears in his eyes that from the time he was a child he had been afflicted with cowardice, and he had joined my captors to prove to himself that he could be brave and courageous. But he found little opportunity to display any bravery or courage. The group of soldiers that he had joined did little in the way of fighting; the towns that they razed offered little or no resistance since the villagers were rarely armed or capable of putting up a fight.

One night I pleaded with him to help us escape. He was reluctant at first, and I do know that part of his reluctance stemmed from his fear of his fellow captors. But strangely, he also confessed that if he helped us escape he would lose me, and with tears in his eyes he said he did not want to be separated from me. Strange

confession of love, delivered in the strangest of circumstances, and made even stranger by the fact that I knew
he realized that he could not possibly expect me to
love him back. But almost with surprise, with the same
sense of amazement that I experienced the first time
I lay with him, I realized how cunning I had become,
how different I was when, while stroking his hair, I lied
to him and told him I loved him. I don't know if he believed me, but perhaps one believes in lies when there
is a need to believe and the truth does not suffice. He
made me promise that we would leave together, and I
agreed.

At night our captors held us with our hands tied behind
our backs, in a tent with a guard at the door. The night
we escaped there was a terrible storm. It was one of
those storms that are typical of this area. It starts with
the sky becoming progressively darker, and the world
becomes silent. I remember that as a child my mother
told me that when the birds stop chirping, the wind dies
down and the night takes over, it's as if the world is
waiting in expectation and fear for God to emerge from
His abode to inspect His world. And when God wanders
about the earth and contemplates His creation, taking
account of the unnecessary suffering, pain and destruction, He cries in anger and frustration, and His tears
are reflected in the rain, His anger in the thunder. And
as one hears the growing thunder and rain one cannot
help but feel sorry for God, who had so much hope and
expectation for humankind, and yet suffers so much dis-

illusionment. And one expects and resigns oneself to the fact that the world will be justifiably destroyed. But in a few hours the thunder dies down and the rain stops, and one realizes that God's anger has abated, and despite His sadness and disappointment, He has decided to return to His refuge and give the world yet one more chance. And thus the sun comes out in all its splendor, and the birds go back to their singing as if celebrating a new beginning, a new undeserved forgiveness.

It was in the middle of this storm that Malus came into the tent, cut our bonds with a knife, and urged us to leave as quickly and quietly as we could. As I exited I saw the guard lying motionless near the door of the tent with blood coming from his mouth, and I understood that Malus had struck him in order to free us. I suppose that it was the only act of courage that he had ever performed. All the prisoners ran out into the nearby forest, and I ran with them. But after walking a few steps I heard my name called out and saw that Malus was following me. And as I turned around to face him, a flash of lightning illuminated our faces, and I saw that he suddenly understood that I had lied to him. His eyes turned cold and angry, and he lifted his arm as if to strike me. But with strength that I did not know I possessed, I pushed him on the chest. He fell backwards, and his head struck a rock. He lay motionless, and I do not know whether I had hurt him or whether he had, out of a last act of kindness, decided to just let me go. I must confess that I hold no affection or endearment whatsoever for that man who in the end probably saved my life and the life of my companions. It is true that in the profound darkness in which we were submerged he reflected light, but it is just as true that in real light he was darkness. This is because although he did not participate in the cruel acts of his fellow captors he remained a bystander to their cruelty, and one who stands idle upon witnessing acts of cruelty is, in essence, cruel himself.

Among the prisoners there was a beautiful young girl, a child, aged no more than twelve, who cried the entire time. She would cry upon awakening and cry herself to sleep. She was not much younger than the rest of the prisoners, but we all tried to console her; despite our efforts, there was no consolation for her. When I left the captors' camp I found the girl sitting and crying at the edge of the forest. I took her hand and dragged her deep into the woods. We were unable to find any of our fellow prisoners, and we walked for hours without seeing a single person. The girl continued to cry, and with each step she seemed to grow weaker. Finally, I literally had to carry her. When she eventually stopped crying I knew that she had died. I know that the cause of her death was sadness, and that each tear contained a fragment of her life, and as her tears fell on the ground, so did the sparkle of her existence. And with the last teardrop, there was no longer any life within her. I had no shovel or strength to build a grave for her and I left her, with her face seemingly at peace, at the base of a giant tree. I hope that someone found her and gave her a proper burial.

I walked for a few more hours, but finally dropped down to the ground in sheer exhaustion. Even though I was terrified at the prospect of being found by my captors, I quickly fell asleep. But in that strange state between wakefulness and sleep I heard a curious sound, a whisper that surrounded me and seemed to softly emanate from the forest around me. Perhaps I was delirious, but what I heard seemed very real. It was a conversation between everything that was alive in the forest- the trees, the animals, the insects. It sounded like a terribly sad but beautiful lament for all of the trees, animals, and everything else in the forest that had perished as a result of the war between men.

And in what appeared to be a beautiful eulogy to the dead, I heard a distinct voice of what I imagined was that of a very old and very large tree, one of the few large ones that remained. It cried out with anger and sadness, denouncing the senseless destruction. It shouted that man is incapable of believing that anything supersedes the importance of his war. War to man is more important than the singing of birds, or the flight of the eagles, or the serene beauty of the jaguar walking through the jungle, or the harmony and order of a world that has existed for millions of years. War is more important than the trees, or the flow of the rivers. And the voice cried out in sadness for the helplessness of the forest. A tree that took hundreds of years to grow, that has withstood storms and floods, is unable to withstand the fire that man ignites in an effort to drive an enemy from the forest. A river that took an eternity to set its course can be forever destroyed by a dam that is only built by man to reach his adversary. For purposes of his war, for the sole reason of destroying him whom he perceives to be his foe, man will, without the least feelings of guilt or respect, destroy forests, rivers, scores of animals, anything in nature that unknowingly and innocently stands in his way. The harmony of nature, an ancient harmony that might appear timeless and eternal, is nevertheless destroyed within minutes by man's vicious act of making war. And from hearing that voice, Storyteller, I know that the death of the jaguar and the giant tree are made so much more painful because the tree and the jaguar, who do not understand war, must ask, must make a desperate attempt before they die to understand the reason for their death; and not finding one, they cry out in anguish.

The Magician

The next morning when I opened my eyes, I saw a strange sight, Storyteller. A man was watching me from a distance, and when I opened my eyes, he directed a beautiful smile at me. At first I was afraid and prepared to run away, but upon studying him further, he did not appear to be a threat. He was dressed in a strange way, with a tall hat on his head and multicolored, ragged clothes. It was easy to tell that one of his legs was longer than the other, and when he walked towards me he did so with difficulty, and with a prominent limp. As he approached me I also could see that he had only three fingers on each hand. He was clearly deformed, and the way he dressed made his deformity even more evident.

He asked me with soothing words not to be fearful of him. When I began to walk, he asked if he could walk with me. I acceded, and while walking by my side he began talking, rapidly at times, and frequently laughed. He explained that he was a magician, a traveling performer who made his living doing magic tricks in front of anybody who stopped to look at him. And when magic tricks did not suffice, he said with a laugh, he would tell fantastic tales of how he had lost the fingers of his hands, or how one of his legs got shorter. In reality he had been born that way, but he believed that people preferred his tales to the truth.

He told me that during his childhood he had suffered much. Both his parents saw his deformity as a tragedy for themselves, and an insult to their honor. His father cruelly blamed his mother for the child's deformity, and she, ashamed of her child and of herself for having given birth to him, assumed that blame. Shortly after the child's birth, she determined that his deformity was a punishment for a sin that she had committed. She was a virtuous woman and was unable to identify a specific event in her past for which she required punishment, but the fact that she could not remember the sin was, in her mind, still further proof of its gravity, and her lack of memory of it a result of her sinfulness. Her desperation to discover the nature of her sin and her constant atonement for an unknown fault in her past consumed much of her energy, to the point that she neglected the care of her child, who precisely because of his deformity was so desperately in need of her love and care. Perhaps she chose atonement because it is much easier to atone than to seek redemption through the exercise of reparative actions. And although she would never admit it to herself, she held a secret anger towards that strange looking boy who had ruined her life and marriage and had been the source of so much unhappiness. So the magician grew up a lonely person in a world that did not want him. He was a constant prey to the jokes and abuses of the children in his town, and nobody made any attempt to relieve the tears of pain and helplessness that watered the ground upon which he walked.

At age eight he was surprised to learn that he was not his parents' only child, as he had believed until then. His mother told him that ten years before the magician was born she had given birth to a baby boy who was afflicted with some of the same deformities that the magician displayed. And as had occurred with the birth of the magician, his parents were disgraced and ashamed of their son. The boy had grown, like the magician, alone and uncared for. But at an early age he expressed an interest in hunting, and in a rare display of apparent kindness, his mother had bought him a shotgun. Shortly afterwards, his mother told him, the boy was found dead in the forest, after using the gun given to him to end his own life.

The discovery that he had a brother who had been born with physical deformities, and like him had suffered the same tribulations, awakened in the magician a number of emotions. For the first time in his life he felt a great deal of compassion for his parents, who had been accursed with the same malady twice, as if once had not been enough. He had never felt any hint of anger toward them, but from that moment he experienced a greater degree of understanding, and thus expected even less from them than he had in the past. This basically amounted to expecting nothing, and in accordance with his expectations, nothing was given. But he also frequently found himself thinking about that brother and would visit his brother's grave, marked by a simple cross in the edge of the cemetery, almost daily. And during those visits he imagined himself walking side by side, holding his brother's hand, telling him of his dreams and fears. And that image, of two deformed persons walking side by side, became his imaginary refuge; because he was, as we all are so many times in our lives, desperately in need of a refuge.

But the consolation provided by the image of a brother that he had never known did not suffice, and at an early age the magician discovered the only force that could possibly relieve his loneliness and sadness: magic. In the strange magical world that he created, grass became food to quench his hunger, leaves on the ground became the most luxurious of beds, and beautiful beings visible only to him became parents and friends that would comfort his sadness and relieve his fears. And upon this discovery of magic, a change took place within him such that he would cry no longer when other children beat him, and a radiance of serenity and peace illuminated his face. The villagers initially viewed his transformation with curiosity, later with laughter and mocking, and finally with a certain degree of respect and even envy. They, who considered themselves sane, were in constant turmoil; while the magician, who in apparent madness would laugh aloud for no reason and talk seemingly to himself, seemed to have found a happiness impervious to loneliness and hunger. And so the villagers became jealous of that fabricated magical happiness that obviously flowered from his madness, but yet seemed no different from the happiness they so much pursued but could not achieve. It came to pass that many asked themselves in bewilderment, "If happiness is possible from madness, what merit is there in being sane?" And when they believed that others were not observing them, some of the villagers approached the magician to ask him the secret of his magic, a secret that he did not know how to divulge.

When at the age of fifteen he decided to leave the town, the villagers briefly thought of asking him to stay.

SILENT SINNERS, SILENT SAINTS

They dared not admit any trace of love for that strange boy who walked the streets laughing and talking to himself, but for a reason that they could not totally articulate they knew that they desperately needed him, if only to remind themselves that happiness was possible, even if inaccessible to them. And so an air of sadness overtook them when the villagers saw the magician, carrying his meager belongings in a small bag, leave forever the town that had been the only world he had even known. But no one among the villagers could swallow his pride and ask the magician to stay, although he assured me that he would have done so if asked.

He began performing magic tricks in public in an effort to extend that magic that had saved him to those who needed it. He did not make much money from his performances; his audiences were too poor to give more than a few coins. But that did not seem to bother him. He proudly thought that magicians were important, because in a place where reality was painful to bear, illusion could alleviate that pain, even if only for a fragment of time. "For example," he told me as he pulled an apple from his hat and handed it to me, "it can for a moment relieve hunger." He considered the trick with the apple one of the most important in his repertoire, but unfortunately, he said with sadness, he could not give away more than a few fruits. But then his voice turned happy again and he said that even without any apples, his tricks made his audience, especially the children, smile and laugh. And he thought that laughter was extremely valuable because it was a temporary diversion from tears. One cannot simultaneously laugh and cry.

He explained that at one time he had a rabbit that he pulled out of his hat during his magic shows. He had taught the rabbit a few simple tricks that seemed to delight the children during his performances. The magician had bought the rabbit as a baby in a market and throughout the years had become quite fond of it. He told me in an embarrassed tone that during his long travels in the countryside, he would often talk to the rabbit, and the rabbit appeared to understand the magician's loneliness. The rabbit had been, in the magician's own words, the best and most loyal of friends that he had ever had.

But once he came to a roadblock and when the soldiers searched him, they took away his rabbit. The magician recounted with tears in his eyes how right in front of his eyes, and laughing at his pleas and cries, a soldier had beheaded the rabbit with a machete and then skinned it to cook it. The magician was heartbroken for months afterwards; even years later he continued to talk to the rabbit as if it were there, and had frequent dreams about the animal.

During the days that we walked the roads to return to my village, the magician rarely stopped talking. His monologue was intermingled with laughter and tears, depending on the subject of his conversation. Once, when he noticed that I scrutinized the road in front of us in fear of meeting my captors, he smiled at me and stated that I should worry no longer- he had used his magic to make the captors disappear forever. I was surprised by his comment because I had not divulged my story to him, but I did not ask him how he knew, and he clearly made no effort to address that question. To onlookers we must have been a strange sight, Mr. Storyteller: a limping man with a tall hat and ragged clothes walking side by side with a barefoot young girl.

When we encountered a town or village on our journey he would find the poorest sections and shout for people to gather and witness his performance. His tricks were simple and common: pulling handkerchiefs from the children's ears or a ball from his hat, or making a coin disappear. But the laughter and joy that he displayed during his performance were more captivating to the audience than were the tricks themselves. And he would always end with the apple trick. With the few coins that he gathered he would immediately buy more apples, which he then gave away in his next show, only keeping a few for us.

When the children, innocent in their cruelty but cruel nonetheless, made fun of his limp and laughingly imitated his gait, or mockingly pointed at his hands, he would exaggerate his deformity even more and laugh along with them, at times so hard that he would bend over in laughter. I never saw him get angry or utter a harsh word; on the contrary, when he saw someone who looked sad he would approach that person and talk to him or her for a few minutes. I do not know what he said to these people, but he always managed to make them smile.

When we finally arrived at my village we parted ways. He did not want to accompany me any farther. As he walked away with his unusual gait and wearing that ridiculous hat, he turned numerous times to smile and wave at me until he had disappeared over the horizon. I have never seen him again, Storyteller, but I have no doubt that I was given a rare opportunity to meet one of God's most beautiful creatures, a much needed "angel in disguise," sent to accompany me on that most difficult of journeys.

The Return

The return to my village was a sad one, Storyteller; of my entire family, only my father remained alive, and he was a broken man. And so was everyone that remained in the village. Everybody recounted in tears the loss of a parent, a child, a sibling. Homes had been destroyed, women raped; senseless suffering, Storyteller, and even more hurtful because of its senselessness.

Shortly afterwards, I realized that I was carrying a child. Because I had never known any other men, I knew that it was from the multiple times that I had been raped while held captive. And Storyteller, it is difficult to convey with words my feelings upon that discovery. I felt horror, amazement, curiosity, gladness, and even doom.

And then a thought entered my mind- a secret message from a merciful God. Gold can be turned to rust, or rust to gold, but one must decide upon one of these options. In other words, Storyteller, beauty can be turned into ugliness, as my captors had done with the life and world of their prisoners. But just as readily, ugliness can be turned into beauty. My child was conceived in the most horrible of circumstances, but I made up my mind that he or she would shine like gold in this world of rust. Although it was not my intention, it was the best possible mode of revenge. My captors' goal had been to inflict pain; instead, they had injected beauty into the life that they had with so much ardor attempted to destroy. And if any beauty could result from the ugliness of my captors, it was in the form of my child, a truth that, sadly enough, they would never realize.

But when my father learned of my pregnancy he became terribly angry. He became even angrier when, in defiance to his order, I refused to have an abortion. In some strange way, so strange that I believe even he could not understand, he blamed me for my pregnancy. With more concern for his honor than for his daughter, he told me that I had to leave his house and depart the village. I learned then a powerful lesson, Mr. Storyteller. Cruelty is expected from the cruel, and while horrific and painful it is not surprising, because we know its source. But cruelty is most intense when it comes from a source we do not expect. And cruelty is the cruelest, it is the most painful, when it comes from those we love and who we know love us back.

I left the village one morning with the few possessions that I had, once again feeling terribly lonely. It was a rainy, dreary day, but surprisingly this fact somehow alleviated my pain; the world seemed to be in harmony, empathizing with my feelings of despair and loneliness. It was all I could do to hold off my tears, but the tears were at the same time of sadness and gratitude. Nobody was present to see me off. But to this day I hold no anger toward my father or to those in the village. I know that in the bottom of their heart they wanted to help and save me. Instead, they committed a grave mistake that I know they regretted for the rest of their lives; they allowed their hearts to be governed by their pride, and one's heart should always be above one's pride.

While I never saw my father again, I do know that my departure caused him great pain, even though it was he who had ordered it. He believed that he was crying for himself, but he was somehow crying for me. Many years after his death, I learned that he had died crying; I wish I had been there to hold his hand and tell him that it had turned out all right; that, considering the circumstances, he had done the right thing. I wish that I had helped him die in peace, because while peace is terribly important, it is most important at the time of one's passing. During the months until my child was born I wandered from village to village. At times I worked in the fields, at times in people's houses, always on the verge of hunger and despair; always jumping from stone to stone, never staying anywhere for long, never being in a place that I could really call home.

The Vegetable Farmer

For a while I worked in the fields of a vegetable farmer. He was a brutish, violent man of gigantic size who remained drunk most of the time and barely cared for his fields. He would spend most of his waking hours in the tavern and then stagger back to his house late at night. Almost daily, when he returned to his house, I could hear the screams of his wife and children as he beat them. In the morning they would emerge with tearful eyes and bruises on their faces, and it was they who worked from dawn to dusk on the farm. The farmer awakened in the afternoon and without saying a word to his family, would return to the tavern.

The farmer's wife was a small, meek woman who spoke little and wore her suffering like one wears a cloak. She had the resigned look of someone who is trapped with no possibility of escape, and it was this resignation rather than the brutality of her husband that was the imaginary, unbreakable chain that kept her constrained. She had so resigned herself to unhappiness that happiness did not seem at all possible. She did not pursue it because she thought it was unattainable, and so every available door that throughout the years had been available to her she had closed from the inside. Many times, she confessed to me, she had thought of leaving her husband, but an unknown force had always thwarted her efforts.

Once I found one of the farmer's children, a beautiful girl no older than twelve, crying in the barn. When she saw me she attempted to hide her tears, only to break down when I held her close to me. She then confessed that she had decided to kill her father, although she did not know how to go about doing it. She asked me not to dissuade her from her decision and not to tell the rest of the family. She wanted no other person to be responsible for her father's death other than herself. She did not care if she was found guilty for his murder; she saw no other way to save her mother and siblings. I frankly did not know how to reply. That same night the farmer came staggering into the barn looking for me. He did not see me, but I knew that from that time on the scene would repeat itself nightly. Images of my former captors came to me and I decided to leave the farm immediately. I felt terribly sorry for the family, but I did not know how I could help them.

A few days later I encountered the farmer's daughter on the road. The sadness was no longer present on her face, and I asked her about her family. She told me that a few days back she had gone into town to buy some supplies and found a crowd circling a magician, a disfigured man who wore a ridiculous hat and performed simple magic tricks. When the crowd dispersed, the magician approached her and asked her the reason for her sadness. She was so surprised by his question that she broke out crying. The magician held her in his arms and she told him everything, all the suffering and pain endured by her family for so many years. In an attempt to console her, the magician told her he would perform a magic trick that would alleviate their suffering.

The next day her father was found dead in the river. The police told her family that they believed he had drowned after falling from the bridge he drunkenly crossed nightly on his way from the tavern to the farm. By a strange coincidence, the magician was also found that same night dead after apparently drowning a hundred feet downstream. Nobody could explain why he would be bathing in the middle of the night. The policeman thought that because of his disfigurement, the magician was not strong enough to fight the current. This explained the multiple bruises on his body presumably made by the rocks as he tried to swim. But as the girl walked away, tears came to my eyes as I realized the magical sacrifice made by a beautiful and terribly vital angel.

The Cathedral

Once, when the fear and despair seemed too much to bear, I went into a cathedral in the middle of the forest. It was a beautiful building made entirely of wood, an oasis of peace and serenity. The pillars were made of huge trees, so large and majestic that I realized that trees of such size no longer existed; they had all been cut down generations ago. The walls were lined with beautiful statues, some made of wood and others of silver and gold. Faint light entered from two windows at each end of the building and hundreds of small candles lit the almost total darkness.

I sat down in a pew in the back and a priest, a young man with very dark skin, approached me. He sat down a few feet from me and for a short time was silent. And then, perhaps noticing the impact that the cathedral made upon me, he began telling me its story. The cathedral, he said, had been built by a proud race of people who had once been the sole masters and inhabitants of this land. Their gods had the face of the jaguar, the color of the forest, the strength of the fire, and the majesty of the sun and moon. But when they showed their idols to the invaders from the strange land from across the sea, they were told they were worshipping the wrong gods. They were told that the real God was simple and poor like they were, but unlike them, who survived on simple food from the forest and lived in houses made of mud and straw, this God needed huge cathedrals, which they would need to build, and statues of gold and silver, which they would have to dig for in mines. A few timidly questioned the obvious contradiction between the God depicted in their paintings, dressed in poverty and rags, and the need for extravagant cathedrals to worship that same God. They even questioned the need for statues of gold and silver, precious metals that that God probably had never known. But those who presented these arguments were said to lack understanding, and those bold enough to insist on an answer were silenced forever. And thus an alien faith was imposed upon them, a faith that quickly enslaved them: a faith in a God who provided little for them, but expected them to sacrifice their sweat and their lives for a building where that same God, simple like them and yet at the same time vain and arrogant, presumably expected to be worshipped. And once they embraced the faith of their captors, chains and whips were no longer needed to imprison them or to force them to work. Faith itself became the chain, and the fear of punishment for their sins in a later life became the whip that drove them to work until they dropped in sheer exhaustion. And the focus of their life, the sole purpose of their existence, became those buildings, and many generations died in their efforts to complete them. And when the cathedral was finally finished, they, the builders, the ones whose sweat and tears were the real cement that held the pillars together, were denied access to it- that being the privilege only of the rich among their masters.

But in the end, the cathedral was not wholly ungrateful to its builders, or at least to a group of their descendants. Almost a hundred years after it was built, a group of villagers from the local town took refuge within its walls. They were escaping from a horde of invaders during one of the thousand wars that afflict this accursed region like an unrelenting illness. A few armed men among the refugees positioned themselves in the cathedral's tower and kept the attackers at bay. However, the limited ammunition and the overwhelming number of attackers made the refugees' position nothing less than hopeless. But afraid of the slight advantage that darkness offered the sharpshooters in the cathedral, the attackers decided to surround the building and renew their attack the next morning.

That night a strange wind blew in the region. It began as a soft breeze, but within a few hours it grew to a magnitude never before remembered by the inhabitants. The multiple legends recalling that event all agree that no one could discern the origin of the wind. It did not come from the north, as the wind usually did in this area, but neither did it originate from any clear direction. Instead, it appeared to originate from all directions at once, or at times, from the earth itself. But despite its magnitude, it did not cause the expected massive destruction; instead, the trees and buildings appeared to be unaffected by it. But when the attackers ventured outside the buildings in which they had taken refuge, they were swayed from side to side by the wind as if they were weightless. In fact, legend recounts that the wind grew stronger the closer the attackers came to the cathedral.

SILENT SINNERS, SILENT SAINTS

When a few days later the wind abated somewhat the attackers left the town, and shortly afterwards the wind finally died down. And thus the refugees were saved, and the tradition from then on was that the cathedral had saved the refugees in gratitude to their ancestors; the sons were saved due to the merit of their fathers.

When the priest stopped talking, I saw that he was quite angry. And then, noticing my stare, he confessed that he was a descendant of the builders, and although a member of the invaders' faith, and perhaps himself enslaved by it, as a young man he had voluntarily joined the monastery that was attached to the cathedral. He had done so partly because he, like his ancestors, held a deep fascination and love for that magnificent building and for all that was contained therein. Little trace remained of that proud race which, before becoming slaves and builders, had been creators of music, art, and legends; and thus the cathedral, ironically built for the invaders, was the only earthly object that linked him to his past. He was prone to nightmares that frequently kept him from sleeping, and on many nights he would arise from his bed and come to the cathedral. And many times, in the twilight between wakefulness and sleep, he believed that he heard the voices of his ancestors issuing from the walls.

The priest's name was John and he seemed to be not much older than myself. He was thin and frail, and he radiated an air of kindness that led me to confide in him. When I told him my story, his face expressed horror and compassion. He offered to talk to the head priest so that I could perhaps work and live in the monastery, and left me waiting in the cathedral while he did so. An hour later he returned with a smile on his face; and this is how I came to spend some of the most peaceful months of my life within those monastery walls.

The monastery consisted of a central courtyard surrounded by the various rooms that the priests used to eat, meditate and sleep. At the center of the courtyard there was a very old and very beautiful fountain, and the water from that fountain was frequently the only sound that was heard. At one time there had been over fifty priests living in it, but now there were only ten, most of them elderly, with John being the youngest member. My work in the monastery was tiring and arduous, but the silence and sense of peace that enveloped that place were so soothing that I did not mind the long hours spent daily cleaning the floors, washing the clothes of the priests, and helping to prepare their meals. And since many of the priests had taken an oath of silence, few words were said between the monastery's inhabitants and myself.

The monastery was a world within a world. When at night its doors were locked and the sound of the fountain was all that could be heard, the outside world, with all that a world could contain, all its beauty and its horrors, that other world seemed so distant, and even more, so unreal, as if it were a dream or an illusion, and the only real world seemed to be the one contained within those monastery walls. And the monastery was proof that man, if he so chooses, is able at times to select the circumstances that surround him, choose among worlds and not fall into the delusion that there is only one, a supposedly real world, that one is forced to reside in. And it is always possible, and at times desperately necessary, to build a monastery, to build walls, even if only around one's heart, to stop the outside world from engulfing us and making us its accomplice. And to some of the priests who had lived in the monastery since they were young boys the monastery was the only world that they had ever known. When they occasionally ventured outside they returned panting, walking as fast as they could, and despite their age, at times breaking into a run like frightened children, as one escaping from a bad dream. One could see the relief on their faces, their frightened hearts caressed and soothed, as they crossed the doors of the monastery.

Part of my work consisted of caring for a very old priest who, as a result of illness, spent much of his day in bed. His room consisted of a tiny dark cell, with only a small window to the outside that barely allowed light to enter. He was one of the only remaining priests who had lived in the monastery since the time it was built, and the others seemed to highly respect him, although they also honored his wish for solitude. Much of the time he kept his eyes closed, and he had only a few words for me when I brought him his meals and helped with his care. But on one occasion he told me the silence had become overwhelming and he needed to talk with me, because what he needed to say could not be heard by his fellow priests. He explained that in these, the last days of his life, he was making an exhaustive recounting of his past. His memory, which had begun to fail him in the months prior to his illness, nevertheless seemed surprisingly agile for this arduous task. He could remember even the smallest of decisions that he had made or failed to make in his lifetime and which had in summation brought him to his present world view.

In this strangest of journeys within his mind he briefly stopped in places where he could have taken a path other than the one he had chosen. And upon the stage of his imagination, finally unrestrained by the fear that had dominated him all his life, with curiosity and boldness he briefly took these paths to see where they would have led him. When he returned from one of these journeys he confessed to me, with tears in his eyes, that he had made some serious mistakes in the course of his life; some of them he could blame on ignorance, or youth, or unavoidable circumstances. But the others, and sadly this was the majority, he could only ascribe to idleness, fear, greed, and worst of all, cowardice. He had always been a cautious man, but he now realized that what he had taken for caution had in reality been lack of courage. And he told me that perhaps the deepest sadness a person can experience stems from looking at one's past and realizing that one has failed to live the life he should have lived.

There was a particular incident, perhaps a wrong choice that he had made, that seemed to distress him the most. He refused to tell me the nature of that event, but its memory consistently brought tears to his eyes. And one day he told me that when, in his mental journeys, he returned to that particular point in time and recalled that particular event, the images became so vivid, and the emotions so real, that he began to wonder whether that event was only taking place in his imagination, or whether he had actually transported himself back to that moment in time, and that he was in fact reliving it. And with that sudden realization, with a new brightness in his voice, he developed a plan: he would return once more to that moment, and this time do what he should have done and make the correct choice in an effort to repair the pain that by his decision at the time he had caused others and himself. But he knew that for this particular journey he would require strength and courage, both of which he continued to lack and which he decided he needed to develop. And thus, for a few weeks he stopped his journeys into the past and forced himself to eat, despite his lack of hunger, so as to gather strength. I do not know what he did to summon courage.

One evening, when I came to withdraw the empty plates of his afternoon meal, he told me that he was now ready. He asked that I close the door behind me and not come in until the next morning. And for several hours from the hall outside of his room I heard sobs, occasional shouting, and at times tearful arguments. The next morning when I entered the room, I found the priest dead in his bed, and the smile and peaceful expression on his face were clear indications that he had been successful in this final and most important of journeys.

There were other priests who, after completing their morning prayers, would sit around the fountain in complete silence, apparently in deep thought. John told me that they were the group of memory seekers. John said that there are those who are unable to understand the true significance of events or experiences that occur to them at the precise time that they take place, and instead are only able to grasp their significance afterwards, when those events have passed and they are viewed as things of the past. These people live their lives through means of their memories, and it is not from present events but only through those memories that they are able to feel any emotions.

I certainly see some clear advantages to living in such a way: because one becomes aware of the importance of events only after they have passed, there is no possibility of acting upon them, and thus, at least initially, no sense of guilt for not having done so when action might have been required. But on the other hand, if an event held a certain degree of beauty, that beauty is also perceived only as a memory and not as an actual emotion accompanying the occurrence of that event. At times they were surprised by the degree of beauty that is contained in events and actions when they are reflected upon, while that same beauty was not seen, or rather not appreciated, in the "here and now" of the event. And they became saddened, even angry, at that missed opportunity to have experienced beauty. Ultimately, in many of them, a sense of sadness slowly emerges, a sense that arises from the realization that too much time was spent thinking about what could have been done, rather than in actually acting.

A few weeks after I came to the monastery, John asked in an urgent tone to speak with me. He told me that in the last few weeks a new sensation, an emotion never before experienced, had grown inside of him and taken over every aspect of his being. At first he had felt a vague sense of restlessness, and he feared that the years of insomnia and nightmares had finally caught up with his frail body and that he was becoming ill. But then it grew into a feeling of excitement, then anguish, and then a sort of happiness, each of these appearing in sequence and then at times all at once. These strange emotions confused him, and as he told me about them he covered his face with both hands, at times sobbing, and at other times giggling like a child. And for the first time in his life the nightmares, which like devilish beings interrupted his sleep for as long as he could remember, had finally left him, but now it was this new sensation that kept him from sleeping. And in a sudden and unexpected movement, John embraced me almost with despair and, sobbing uncontrollably, confessed that it was I who was the cause of those emotions. Almost shouting, he told me that he had fallen in love with me.

I must admit that I have never experienced those emotions described by John, and I have often wondered, perhaps with a degree of envy and curiosity, what it would be like to feel them. I loved my family in my youth, and I later grew to love my child enormously, but I have never loved in the manner that John confessed he loved me. And when I told this to John he looked at me in silence, almost in disbelief, and without uttering another word he walked away.

Two nights later I heard a faint knocking, almost like a scratching on the door of my cell, and when I approached the door I heard John pleading with me to let him enter. For a moment I thought of allowing him in, because by that time, after the multiple times that I had been raped, I considered my body to hold no virtue, and it would have been so easy to relieve the pain and torment caused by John's unfulfilled desire for me. But I knew that it would not have been that simple. If I had allowed John entrance into my cell, I would also have had to allow him entry into my heart, and my heart remained sealed to him- it held no doors that could be opened by any man. So I kept the door closed, and in my mind I could see John, his head on his chest and resignation in his heart, walk away in tears. The next morning he was nowhere to be found. He had apparently left the monastery during the night, and many months later I learned from one of the priests that I encountered on the road that he had never returned. I often wondered whether the cause of his departure was the disappointment caused by my rejection, or the excitement caused by the new emotions that he had discovered within himself and that he could only hope to experience again outside the world of the monastery.

After John's departure, something changed in the monastery. A building absorbs and reflects the essence irradiated by those who live, work and love within it, and it is not the same without them. And I suppose that part of the peace and harmony that I had experienced in the monastery had stemmed from John's presence. A few weeks later, when my pregnancy began to show and the time of delivery approached, the head priest asked me into his office and told me I had to leave the monastery. The baby could not be born within its walls. He said this with a certain degree of apology and sadness, but I was not at all angered by his request. And so the next day, carrying in a small bag all that I owned, I jumped to yet another stone. As I looked back from the road to the monastery, I felt a deep sense of gratitude toward that building and its inhabitants, who along with their silence and serenity had provided me so much kindness and peace.

Daniel Drubach

The Old Man

One day I encountered an old man sitting on the ground by the road. He did not turn his head toward me when I approached but instead looked directly in front of him with a blank stare. As I got close to him, he put out his hand and asked me for food, but when I replied that I had nothing to give him, he gave me a broad smile and told me that when I had spoken he had seen the most beautiful colors, especially blues and greens. Curious about his answer, I asked him to explain what he meant. He told me that he had lost his sight a few years back, and since that time he occasionally saw colors in his mind when he heard voices. And when this happened he could deduce more about the person who had spoken from the colors that he saw than from the sound of that person's voice. And in the array of colors that he saw in his mind, the green, the blue and the purple were especially important and beautiful.

He asked me to sit by him and he told me his story. He did not know the disease that had caused his blindness, but his vision had deteriorated over the course of several months, and on the day that he was unable to distinguish between day and night he was devastated, and cried for several days. He initially thought that he could conceive of a life without sounds, touch, or taste, but the thought of being unable to see terrified him greatly. But as he slowly became accustomed to his world of darkness, he realized, with a great deal of amazement, that he now was able to perceive certain things that he could not when he had been able to see. And he discovered that it was precisely his sight, his ability to see, that had prevented him from perceiving things invisible to the eyes. There was, for example, a very soft noise, almost like a hum, that seemed to come from many objects in the universe that surrounded him. Certain stones, trees, clouds, and even the ground itself in certain places emitted that hum. He was not yet able to understand its meaning, but he believed that it was a conversation, some sort of communication between all that produced this sound. He had grown to believe that everything in the universe somehow communicated with everything else, and man, perhaps because of his vision, is excluded from that conversation.

And as the darkness that slowly engulfed him became more profound, he began to perceive a wondrous light. It was a very special type of light, one that he perceived led to deep understanding. With that light one not only could see a particular event, but also immediately see and understand the circumstances that had led to that event, and comprehend its consequences as well. It was a light that illuminated the past, present and future, so that all three could be seen simultaneously, without the mental barriers that we place between them. And with that light he could see everything, and everyone's place and purpose in the order of the universe. And once the old man fully appreciated the significance of that light he became terrified by it. He thought that no man should be privy to that type of knowledge, that he would not be able to withstand its weight. But no matter how much he tried, he could not dim the intensity of that illumination, could not close his eyes to it, because that light did not come to him through his eyes. And he even tried to gaze directly at the light, in the hope that its intensity would blind him, as a man who looks at the sun becomes blinded by its radiance. After that failed, he even contemplated committing suicide, because the light utterly overwhelmed him, but with time he became resigned to it. And his terror was somewhat relieved after he realized that along with the power to utilize that light, he had also been given the choice not to use it. And thus he would only see if he chose to look, and he decided to refrain from looking.

But after making that resolution, a certain restlessness came to possess him, one which tormented him every night. He wondered if he should use that light to illuminate his own life, to discover its meaning and purpose, to understand the circumstances that had led him to where he was now standing, and to gaze at his future. But he was afraid of what he would discover, and every time he had the urge to gaze, he had been able to stop himself. But he was afraid of his growing weakness, and he knew that one day, and he hoped it would be the day of his death, he would use that light.

And I must confess, Storyteller, that as I listened to the old man, I also had the urge to ask him, to plead with him to use his special power to look into my life, so that

I could make sense of so much senselessness. But like him I was also afraid of what I would learn or discover. And thus, I did not ask him.

Adam

I continued my wandering in search of work and food. And then, in the middle of the seemingly unending storm that my life had become, the sun suddenly emerged in the form of Adam, a boy who was born to me in the early spring. Words are not enough to describe either Adam or the beautiful brightness that he brought into my wretched life. I named him Adam, because he was to be the father of a new generation, a new type of human who would abhor war and seek peace, a new hope for the world. He was a quiet, gentle boy, frequently alone, but seemingly in peace. He had the beautiful ability to put himself in the place of other human beings, no matter who they were. When they were in pain, he would feel their pain. When they felt joy, he felt joy and celebrated for them, even if they themselves did not know it. He ascribed feelings- joy and sadness- to plants and animals, and made himself feel what he thought they felt. He would be careful not to pull a branch from a tree, or strike an animal, or kill an insect, thinking of the pain that this would cause. And wild birds would approach him, at times even perch on his arms, because they knew that Adam would not hurt them. And Adam would laugh, a beautiful laugh that sounded like clear water running down a mountain stream, a laugh that would mix with the chirping of the birds, as if they were laughing with him. Rust to gold, Mr. Storyteller; I know nothing about his father, but nothing in Adam reflected the rust that had brought about his existence.

I remember one day I found him crying inconsolably. He told me that it was due to something he had seen at the fair a few minutes before. A traveling performer held an old bear at the end of a rope. The bear was an old, scrawny and dirty animal whose teeth had been brutally extracted when he was a cub so that he would be unable to bite his owner. Despite this he was muzzled at all times, which further added to his pitiful humiliation. His coat was in a poor state, patchy and full of lice. He scratched almost constantly, and during his performance his owner would punish him for doing so with a sharp blow to his nose with a wooden stick. The performances were nothing less than pathetic. His master would play a tune on the accordion, and the bear, rising on his hind legs, would move around as if he danced. And the audience seemed enchanted by this sad demonstration and clapped loudly. But only Adam was able to recognize the suffering and humiliation, the terrible longing for freedom and for a life with meaning reflected in the bear's eyes. This was the reason for Adam's tears. He asked me, with desperation in his voice, whether I would help him free the animal from his master and his suffering. And as I held Adam tightly to my chest, I wondered how I could tell a crying child with a beautiful heart, a child not yet ten years of age, how I could make him understand, that on this strange world, with few exceptions, the strong prey on the weak, and the weak on those weaker than they, on down to those who are so weak themselves that they lack the strength to prey on others.

Despite the beauty and happiness that Adam brought into my life, he also represented another mouth to feed, and it became more difficult to make enough money working in the fields. The war had ended and there was hunger all around us. One day, after several days of hunger and desperate attempts at finding any type of work, a man offered me money if I slept with him. And this is, Storyteller, how I became a prostitute. I must confess that at the time I felt no shame. Nothing else mattered except providing food for Adam.

A few weeks later Adam came back to the shack that had become our temporary home with bruises covering his entire body and with his clothes torn. He initially refused to disclose what had happened to him, but after much pleading he admitted that he had gotten into a fight with a group of boys much older than he. He bravely held back his tears as he refused to confess his reasons for fighting, but later he admitted that the group of boys had called him a bastard, and that they had made derogatory comments about me because I was a prostitute. His anger made him fight desperately, but he could do little against the large group of boys who finally knocked him unconscious.

I remember that, after he fell asleep, I cried much that night. My tears were not for myself, for whom I felt no pity, but for Adam, whose cruel destiny was to have a prostitute for a mother, through no fault of his own. And for the first time, Storyteller, I became ashamed of what I had become. And as I thought of Adam, a frail boy of ten, fighting against a large group of boys much older than himself in an attempt to defend his mother's honor, I realized that this was the greatest display of courage that I had ever known. And I lay awake that night wondering what I would say to Adam the next morning, how I would explain the reason for what I had become. But I did not have an opportunity to do so, Storyteller. The next morning Adam acted as if nothing had happened and did not wait to listen to any explanations -an act of mercy, Storyteller: he did not allow me to humiliate myself.

But I had to jump to another stone in the river, Mr. Storyteller. Adam died in my arms when he was a few days over ten years old. He had always been a frail child, a product of constant hunger and of unending marches in search of work and food. He contracted a fever that no healer or doctor could cure, despite my desperate attempts to do whatever was necessary to buy him the medicines that they prescribed. During the last five days of his life he was delirious, drifting from wakefulness to sleep. He would often burst out crying, and once when without success I did all I could to comfort him, he confessed that his greatest fear of dying was not of death itself, but of leaving me alone in this world. He asked me over and over, between inconsolable sobs, how I would manage without him. I just held him tight and did not know what to say, because in truth, I could no longer conceive of a world devoid of his laughter, his kindness, his words, his beautiful presence. And I did not know how to lie to him.

When he finally became unable to speak he looked at me with eyes that asked and said so much. He was fighting death with all the strength that his frail little body would allow him, and I knew that the only reason he kept battling was because of me. As everything in his life had been, even his final fight, a hopeless battle with death, was an act of kindness. I prayed for death to conquer, because I realized that his hold on life was a painful struggle, and I so much wanted him to be at peace. As the days went by his eyes would remain closed for longer periods of time, and one day, with me holding him tight so that neither of us would be alone, he gave his last breath. I don't understand the reason for his death, Storyteller. I suppose that there was a shortage of angels in heaven, and his presence was required with greater urgency there than on this earth. But Storyteller, I needed him so much.

When I carried his body to the church, the priest refused to bury him in the church cemetery because, as he said, "he had been conceived in sin." I was so saddened by my grief that I had no energy to argue with him. Stupidity, Mr. Storyteller, knows no boundaries. No matter how much sin was contained in Adam's conception, it made no sense to blame that sinfulness on him. And Mr. Storyteller, despite all that I have gone through in my life, I continue to believe in a merciful God. And I do think that the essence of religion, its beliefs and moral codes, is a precious diamond which projects beautiful light. However, we humans throughout the ages have taken that diamond and built multiple walls and structures in order to protect it, but those same buildings have become so intricate and complex that we have forgotten how to navigate within them in order to reach the very object that they are meant to guard. And thus we are frequently no longer able to see the light from the diamond, and instead can only see the walls. And this explains why the priest, a good and pious man, but bound by the laws within his faith, would not allow Adam's burial in the church grounds.

Adam was buried outside but immediately adjacent to the cemetery walls, and thus on ground that was not sacred. But a curious and beautiful event occurred. In time, the cemetery became too small to hold the dead. When it was enlarged, Adam's grave came to rest within its new walls. I call this a beautiful event because so much beauty is contained in seemingly chance occurrences, and it is a sad privation for a person to ignore this rare opportunity to experience beauty.

SILENT SINNERS, SILENT SAINTS

And subsequently I died again, from a life that had commenced with a brutal rape, continued with the birth and life of a beautiful child, and ended with his death. And if it would be possible to quantify sadness, longing and despair, then I had, with Adam's death, reached the most that could be possible. Since Adam's death I have not been able to love, Mr. Storyteller. I suppose that all the love that was contained within me I gave to him, and I have none left to give to anyone else, not even to myself. Adam took my love to his grave where it lies next to him, comforting him perhaps.

And that, Storyteller, is how I reached my present state. Since I had lost everything that was important to me, I had nothing left to lose. And being a prostitute means that in the eyes of society I am the lowest of the low. But I am no longer angered by the looks of reproof and disgust that some direct toward me when I walk the streets. This is especially so for the women, who more often than not cross the street when they see me coming. And Storyteller, my way of life has taught me how much hypocrisy rules human existence. The same men who lie with me at night will look at me with anger and reproof during the day. A judge who, after making a long and passionate discourse in the courtroom about the importance of virtue and modesty, prior to sentencing me to jail for a few days, is the same man who weekly seeks out my services.

But occasionally, and only occasionally, someone will give me a smile, or a pat on the shoulder, as if understanding the circumstances that have brought me to my present state. Only a few possess that kind of vision, to see people in their current state and guess, or at least consider, the circumstances that brought them to that condition, and thus incorporate this into their judgment. And I am so thankful for those small and effortless, yet vitally important, acts of kindness.

And if for a moment, Storyteller, you are willing to believe me, being what I am has allowed me to provide a bit of help to the world that surrounds me. Many men come to me for a temporary respite from their loneliness and despair. Some come only to talk, others to be able to cry, which is not allowed to them in their homes. Many of them, after making love, lie by my side just sighing, staring into space, making an account of their past and present lives, and some leave having made new resolutions, new promises to themselves. Most leave with a lighter heart and some with rediscovered hope. I never talk to any man who lies by my side, because my silence gives him room to talk, or to think. And some have told me that in my silence they find an answer to many of their questions, an answer which had lain dormant within them, but is now allowed to spring into the light because there is somebody to listen. Some of these men are so consumed by despair and loneliness that it does not take much effort to provide, if even for a moment, a sense of serenity and hope. This is because, Storyteller, a small candle, a small amount of light, can dissipate a lot of darkness.

And being in low places, in the lowest of situations, gives one a rare opportunity if one is willing to take it, Storyteller. Because if one wants to raise another from the mud and the filth, it is often not enough to stand on top and reach down to give him a helping hand. Sometimes it is necessary to climb all the way down to him, into the filth and the mud that entraps him. Only then can one take hold of the other with strong arms and pull him into the sunlight.

And that, Storyteller, is the end of my story. I can tell that it saddened you, but Storyteller, do not feel pity for me because I do not feel it for myself. And in truth, all things beautiful that were taken away from me, before being taken away, had been given to me. And for that, for the gifts despite the losses, I am thankful. Even my life, Storyteller, was a gift, because my parents in the village were not my true parents. When I was an infant my parents and brothers were killed by a group of bandits when they robbed our family while crossing the desert. This is a shame, Storyteller, because my father was a shoemaker who had little to be robbed of. My life and the life of a brother were spared because of a soldier who, I was told, single-handedly fought the bandits. I have never met that soldier, although I would have liked to, if only to meet a courageous person in a world which I have found to be so full of cowards, a life saver in a world of killers and bystanders. I have also never known that brother; after we were rescued different families adopted us. I have often wondered what that brother was like, and along with the magician, that brother has been at times an imaginary source of desperately needed refuge. If only, Storyteller, I could find him.

[Storyteller's note: If only she could find him! She had been looking right at him! If only I could have followed her and explained. But I had no time to do so because with the end of her story the haze, the mist, whatever it was, cleared; and the old bartender and I sat alone in the bar. Where had she gone? I shook my head and turned to him. "Was it real?" I asked, "Were those people really here? Did they really exist?"

He stared at me with a smile on his face for a few moments and said, "Your outlook is limited. It would perhaps be helpful if I myself now told you a story or two. They might serve to clear things up for you a bit; you must be made aware of the true breadth and depth of the reality in which we live our lives. My first story is about a miracle while my second is about magic. The two stories are similar in that they are both concerned with the nature of life...and death." So saying, he began the first of his stories.]

Miracle
(The Bartender's First Story)

When it began, it was only a light drizzle, nothing more than a slight inconvenience to the multiple merchants selling their produce and wares at the fair held every Sunday in the streets surrounding the village square. But when the rain did not stop after two hours, the merchants closed their stalls and went home. They were not greatly disappointed; the rain had started almost at noon and they had sold most of what they had by that time. In truth, the rain gave them an excuse to go home to their families and even perhaps take a well-deserved nap before lunch. The young married couples were especially glad, since many believed that there was a special delight (and even increased fertility) in making love when it was both daylight and raining, and especially before the midday meal.

When the rain had not abated by nighttime, some of the villagers were surprised. It was the dry season, and while short showers were not unheard of, persistent rain was extremely unusual. And when by morning the rain had not only persisted, but had in fact increased in intensity, some of the older villagers became concerned.

But aside from a few old men who periodically could be seen at the doors of their houses worriedly looking at the sky, the rain put most of the villagers in a festive mood. The downpour made it impossible to work the fields, and the town's inhabitants resigned themselves to an unexpected day of rest. Some of the children ventured out of their houses to play in the rain, holding their faces to the sky so as to fill their mouths with the cool water. The young married couples walked hand in hand to the door of their houses, put out their free hands to feel the rain, looked at the sky, gazed sheepishly at each other, and returned to their lovemaking.

The following day the rain continued. By now the drops of water were large and heavy, and the rain came down with some force. Some of the villagers, seeing no end to the downpour, put on their wide-brimmed hats and went out to work the fields. The rain had turned the dirt streets into deep mud, and in some places their feet sank down to their ankles. The fields were also muddy and slippery, and after a few hours of fruitless labor, the villagers returned discouraged to their homes.

But by the next morning the rain had stopped. The sky remained dark and cloudy, but by midmorning a ray of sunlight could be seen at a distance emerging timidly but determinedly through the clouds. Laughing and excited, the villagers hurriedly left their homes and went about their business. The children went to the schoolhouse dressed in their school uniforms, walking in groups and talking loudly among themselves. The respite in the rain made the earth absorb some of the water that had accumulated in puddles in various sections of the road, and the ground was now as soft as a bed of feathers.

By nightfall the clouds had moved away and the sky was amazingly clear. No one could remember such a beautiful sky. The moon was full and bright and thousands, if not millions, of stars were visible as far as the eye could see. Most of the villagers walked out of their houses and stared at the sky for long periods of time, as though mesmerized by its majesty and beauty. There was yet another local tradition: that lovemaking was especially delightful when there was a full moon, and the young couples were once more seen walking silently hand in hand into their houses.

The next morning it began raining once more, a light and gentle drizzle that seemed to caress with tenderness the uncovered faces of the villagers who walked the streets and fields. But when darkness set in that evening, the villagers witnessed a strange phenomenon: the drops of water seemed to shine with a curious glow. Some reflected the color of silver, and yet others the color of gold. Several of the villagers excitedly carried pots and pans into the streets hoping to collect some of the gold and silver falling from the sky, but they were greatly disappointed when they saw that only water, transparent and clear, filled their wares. And so, wearied by the excitement caused by the events of the last few days, the villagers fell into a deep and restful sleep.

On the day of the gold and silver rain, a student in the school respectfully approached the office of the schoolmaster and knocked on the door. The student reported that the town priest was at the entrance to the school asking to see him. The schoolmaster dismissed the student and went himself to greet the priest.

The schoolmaster was a stern but kindly man who had dedicated his entire life to the education of the town's children. It was a thankless task that provided him barely enough to survive, but his needs were few and he was content with his lot. He had never married, and he led a lonely life, which he did not particularly dislike. Over his lifetime he had developed a very close friendship with the town priest, and that friendship was perhaps one of the most important highlights of his life. Every week they would spend long hours talking over tea and biscuits, discussing a wide range of topics. They knew each other as only two very old friends could, and loved each other dearly.

When he saw the priest standing outside the door, the schoolmaster knew that something was deeply affecting his friend. This was not at all unusual, since the priest was frequently rocked by internal turmoil. During the time that he had spent in the seminary, the idea of heaven and hell had been so pounded into him that the priest spent much of his life worrying about the after-death fate of himself, and especially of his congregants, whom he truly loved. His sermons were endless and repetitious monologues about the beauties of heaven and the horrors of hell, and since most of the congregants knew them by heart, many of the church attendees utilized the Sunday Mass to catch up on much needed sleep. The silence of the church, only broken by the sad and monotonous voice of the priest, was the perfect lullaby to induce the dreams of the villagers.

But when he sat in the schoolmaster's office, it was obvious that the cleric was unusually excited. The priest told him that the previous night he had had a dream, or perhaps a vision, because he was not sure whether he was awake or asleep when he had it. The experience was so vivid, he had for a moment wondered whether it came from God.

The schoolmaster knew that his friend had been, for much of his life, awaiting a message from God. On many sleepless nights the priest had pleaded with God for a word or a sign- some acknowledgment that God, high in heaven, was aware of the lowly priest down on earth. He pleaded for such a sign as a man who has just crossed the desert, exhausted and thirsty, pleads for a glass of water. He had never doubted God's existence, but he had always wondered whether the life he was living, fully dedicated to the service of God, met with His approval. And among his wide array of fears, the one that stood out among the rest, like a gigantic mountain surrounded by low hills, was that at the end of his life he would discover that he should have lived differently. And what a terrible discovery that would be.

Excitement almost beyond containment was in his voice as the priest related his dream- his vision. A saintly woman, one who had quietly and humbly dedicated her entire life to acts of saintliness, who had washed the feet of the poor, fed the hungry, and washed the wounds of those with leprosy, a woman of few words but of innumerable acts of kindness, a beautiful woman who had lived on bread and water most days of her existence so that others could have her food, was about to walk through the village on the way to her home. That angel of skin and bones, feeling in her heart that the time of her death was approaching, realizing that she could do no more for the abandoned children, and the destitute, and the hungry and the sick, had for once in her life wanted something for herself. She wished to return, before the time of her death, to the place where she had been born and which she had left so many years ago as a child, after the death of her parents. And she had decided to return after her parents, in a dream, had called to her to lie next to them, so that they would be able, at least in death, to provide her with the refuge that she had given to so many and had never had herself. And as had been the way of the saintly woman her entire life, taking for herself barely enough to survive and nothing else, so that others could have what she did not need, she accepted nothing for her journey, and set out walking.

But God in His abode, feeling great love and admiration for that saintly woman, wanted so much to ease the journey which He knew would be her last. And He realized that whatever He did would need to be without her knowledge- a hidden miracle; because if she knew, she would insist there were others more needy of His help. And what could God do to ease the journey of a saintly woman who needed so little and expected nothing? God knew that after decades of endless work, the woman could barely lift her feet off the ground when she walked, and that the stones on the dirt roads hurt her feet. And He knew that her feeble eyes were barely able to make out the road. And God realized that a woman that could hardly walk or see would be an easy prey to the many dangers of the road.

And so God made it rain, so that the water softened the roads, which during the dry season were so hard this time of year. And thus the soft roads caressed the woman's feet and made it easier for her to walk. And God put a ray of light inside each raindrop because He knew that, in her eagerness to reach the home of her childhood, the saintly woman would walk even at night. And that lighted rain made it easier for those saintly eyes to see. And to address the dangers of the road, God gathered the only two wolves that remained in the region, sole survivors of a proud species that had for thousands of years roamed the forests and jungles, a species that had been decimated by generations of cruel and useless hunting by man. And God gathered those two magnificent animals, looked into their beautiful eyes and explained the gravity of their mission and they understood, despite the fact that they held no love for man. Even though they did not understand cruelty, they did understand the importance and beauty of kindness.

And God knew that even the most powerful of human kings, even those with the largest of armies and the fiercest and most loyal of warriors, would not be as well protected and guarded as would the saintly woman by those beautiful animals that, unbeknownst to her, protected her with their lives. And as a special act of kindness, knowing that the saintly woman loved the beauty of the sky, God called upon the planets and the stars and asked them to shine their brightest, as they had never done before, on the night when the woman, exhausted from a day of walking, lay to rest for a few hours in an open field.

And after the priest was afforded this vision in his dream he was surprised to discover that God, high in heaven, requested the help of a lowly priest down on earth. He turned to God and said, "Here I am. What do you want me to do?"

It was customary for him to lock the church at night, more from habit than from concern for its safety. God asked him to keep the doors open on the night following the vision. The saintly woman was due to pass through the village that night, and she would want to stop in the church to pray. And God also asked the priest to light candles in the church before he retired for sleep, so that she could see. He reminded the priest that he should do nothing to reveal to the woman the secret miracle.

As the dream began to fade, the priest desperately called out to God, "Please God, before you go, please tell me: am I living my life the way you want me to? Am I doing what I am supposed to be doing?" And God smiled at the priest and with tenderness in His voice He answered, "Yes, you are doing what you were placed on the earth to do. And I am proud of you, and thankful." And then God turned away and the priest returned from his vision.

When the priest finished talking, the schoolmaster was visibly moved, and tears came to his eyes. He had never given much credence to visions or dreams, and he certainly did not believe in miracles. He also did not believe there was any miraculous aspect to the strange events of the recent days. For example, there was sure-ly a scientific explanation for the silver and golden rain;

145

perhaps it was the angle of the light upon the raindrops.

But he was moved because, by looking at the priest, he realized that his friend had achieved his life's quest: he had been talked to by God. The schoolmaster, who viewed himself as a man of science, did not for a moment believe that God had talked to the priest, but he knew that the priest believed so, and he was happy for his friend, who could now die in peace. And putting his arms over the priest's shoulders, he escorted him back to the church, and the doors were left open that night. And the schoolmaster helped the priest light a hundred candles that evening, so that they would remain lit until morning.

The priest lived in a small house across the street from the church. From a small window in the front room the doors of the church were visible. The priest remembered that in his dream God had asked him to do nothing that would reveal to the saintly woman the nature of the miracle. But the priest saw no harm in being a witness to what he thought would be the most important spectacle of his life. So as nightfall approached, he pulled a chair by the window that faced the church. He was determined to remain awake all night if necessary. Nevertheless, before long a profound tiredness overtook him. He did all he could to remain awake, but despite his heroic efforts he fell into a deep sleep. The sun was high in the sky when, surprised and disappointed, he awoke the next morning.

There was only one two-story house in the village; all of the others were built with only a ground floor. It was located at the edge of town and was inhabited by a family of modest means- a couple and their twelve-year-old daughter. The parents slept on the ground floor, while the daughter occupied the only bedroom on the second floor. The upstairs room had large windows that allowed the daughter a magnificent view of the main street of town and the nearby fields.

On the night of the gold and silver rain the daughter awoke and was unable to return to sleep. A strange restlessness, something that she had never experienced before, a feeling that something extraordinary was about to happen, had disturbed her sleep. She could hear the heavy breathing of her parents downstairs and knew that they were in a deep slumber. She thought of awakening them, but unsure of what she would tell them, she sat by the window that gave her a view of the road leading into town. The rain continued to fall, and the silver and gold raindrops created a spectacle that was mesmerizing.

Suddenly she witnessed an event that she would remember her entire life. What looked to be a very large dog, the likes and beauty of which she had never before seen, came trotting down the road into town. For a moment the child wondered whether the animal was a wolf; she had never seen one, but she had learned in school that they had once inhabited the region. Periodically the animal seemed to pause and look behind him, as though he knew he was being followed. And then, trotting from one side of the road to the other and looking about him with watchful eyes, the animal disappeared from her sight, deep into the main street of the village.

A few minutes later the child saw on the road in the distance a small and stooped figure, covered from head to toe in rags, walking toward the town. It walked with a slow and limping gait, holding a cane in the right hand. And when the person passed in front of the house, the child almost cried out in astonishment. Despite the fact that it was raining, the figure, which appeared to be an old woman, seemed to be completely dry. It was as if she walked in the middle of a circle in which the rain did not fall. And a few feet behind her the rain stopped altogether, as though it fell only for her benefit. She walked past the child's house and entered the church a few doors down the road. A few seconds later a second animal, somewhat smaller than the first, perhaps also a wolf, apparently following the old woman from a distance, appeared on the road into the town. It stopped for a moment in front of the church and then trotted to the side of the building and disappeared from the child's line of sight.

The child, amazed to the point of speechlessness by this strangest of processions, was about to run downstairs to awaken her parents when she saw the door of the church open and the old woman walk out. Without turning her head, the woman continued her slow and difficult walk toward the opposite end of town. It continued to rain around her, but not on her. A few seconds later the wolf emerged from the side of the building and followed her.

The child, now awakened from the trance that enveloped her, ran down the stairs to her parents' bedroom. Such was the excitement in her voice that her parents had difficulty understanding her when they were awakened from sleep by her shouts. When she told them about the procession they looked at each other confusedly. And then the mother held the child in her arms and tried to convince her that it had all been a dream. But upon the child's almost desperate insistence, all three went to the front door and looked out. It had stopped raining, and a profound silence enveloped the town. The streets were empty.

For years afterward, the child continued to insist on the veracity of what she saw that night. Strangely enough, it was the town priest who seemed to most believe her. Many times he asked the child to recount the event, and would frequently ask her to search her memory for additional details of that night.

It became clear to the villagers that from the time of the silver and golden rain a profound change had come over the priest. He now radiated a sense of peace and calmness- a sharp contrast from his previous state of irritability and worry. The villagers, who truly loved their priest, saw the change in him as a miracle brought about by the rain. And almost exactly nine months later, over fifteen children were born within a period of two weeks in the village. People remembered the rain and the young lovers, and the children became known as "the children of the rain."

[Storyteller's note: Upon finishing his story, the bartender resumed his smile. "A beautiful story," I said, "and if it is true, I would love to know how you came to know it!"

"Say nothing yet," he said, "but let me continue with the second." He immediately launched into his second story while I sat back wondering how it could ever match his first.]

Soledad
(The Bartender's Second Story)

In a small village there lived a girl named Soledad. Her parents never knew that the name they gave her was to act as a curse, or perhaps a premonition, for the way in which she was to live her entire life. Orphaned at an early age, with not a soul to care for her, she was taken in at the age of nine as a cleaning worker in the home of a wealthy villager. Soledad grew up in silence; the warm radiance of childhood never for a moment illuminated her face. The daily exhausting work, combined with unrelenting solitude and resignation, stole from her any sign of physical beauty that she may have ever been blessed with. She was a lonely, sad child with no other refuge but the universe of her imagination. And there she would frequently run, as quickly as her thoughts would take her, gasping for air, desperately fearful at times that she would not make it in time, and that its doors would close before she could enter. And what would she do then, trapped in a world that held no beauty, no magic, no consolation, no caress for a crying heart?

At the age of thirteen a sparkle of light, timid and trembling, penetrated her darkness. It took the form of a farm boy who weekly delivered goods to her master's house. Desperate for a trace of love, she held on to him as a shipwrecked man hangs on to a floating log. But he repaid her love by brutally raping her one day behind a barn. Without making any attempt to console the terrified and crying child, he simply walked away, disappearing from her life forever.

Two months later she realized that she was carrying a child. For a few days she had been vomiting and clutching her abdomen, and an old cook who questioned and examined her gave her the news without ceremony or emotion. Soledad greeted this announcement with some initial confusion; in a few hours, however, her perplexity turned into happiness. But the old cook did not in the least share her joy. She flatly told Soledad that if the master were to find out, he would have no qualms about putting her out on the street; she had no other choice but to end the pregnancy.

Upon hearing the old cook's statement, Soledad's body and face contracted as if struck with sudden great pain. The life that she now knew was within her was calling to her; she could not forsake it. Because she understood the pain of abandonment, she could not bear to abandon. The old cook, her heart suddenly softened, her eyes unexpectedly moist with tears, looked intently into Soledad's eyes. Many years previously, almost an eternity ago, the old cook herself had been presented with that choice. And a sensation of profound admiration, of sadness for a life wrongly lived, of an intense yearning for a second chance overtook her, and she embraced Soledad almost with desperation and fury, as she had never embraced anyone before. Soledad held the old woman in her arms and lovingly stroked her hair, talking soothingly to her until she stopped crying. And with words coming from outside her, as if someone else were saying them, Soledad heard herself saying, "You have atoned enough." And the old woman considered what a strange world it was; a child barely thirteen had become a temporary sanctuary, a fleeting shelter that she would have thought no longer possible for someone who at the end of her life had lost all hope of redemption.

The following weeks were full of magic. Soledad constantly spoke to her unborn child as if he were there in front of her. Within her was the remedy for her loneliness, the only available resting place for the immense love she held within her, but that until now had been like a bird flying above flooded land, with no branch upon which to rest its weary wings.

When the master of the house found out about her pregnancy and angrily told her to leave, Soledad's bliss was not in the least diminished. She packed her meager possessions and went to live in a rundown and dirty shack at the edge of town. She continued working long hours cleaning houses, and frequently had to walk long distances in order to do so. At night she would arrive at her shack exhausted, too tired to partake of her meager meals.

But a frail body and unrelenting hard work conspired against the child's life, and the baby was born prematurely in the dirty and disorderly shack two months before it was due. It only survived a few hours in Soledad's arms; but regardless of whether it lasts an hour or a century, a lifetime is, to the one who lives it, the only chance to experience the fabric of life. And in truth, we can never hope to know how much a newborn child is cognizant of the world around him, or of the emotions that encircle him. But if the tenderness and love contained in an entire universe could somehow be collected in a bottle, then it was precisely during those brief hours of the child's lifetime that the bottle was gently emptied. No love is as strong as that which accumulates within a lover for a lifetime and finally finds an object or destination upon which it can come to rest, like a weary traveler coming home after a long and treacherous journey.

And I am so much hoping that the child was able to feel that love which was shed on him throughout his short lifetime, because despite its brevity, he would have experienced the very best that life has to offer. And if that was the case, then he was indeed a fortunate child, because far too many children with much longer lifetimes are not so privileged.

SILENT SINNERS, SILENT SAINTS

The child was buried in the small cemetery behind the village's only church. An old carpenter, feeling compassion for a child desperately crying for the death of another child, built a casket so small that it seemed to have been made to hold a pair of shoes. Except for the town priest and the gravedigger, no one other than Soledad was present at the funeral. It was raining, and the drops of water that fell on Soledad's face became one with her tears; and it seemed that the sky was also crying, saddened not only by the death of a child, but saddened even more by the tears of the child's mother.

After the child's death, Soledad sunk into a deep state of melancholy. She would rarely leave her shack, and if not for the old cook who daily brought her leftover meals from the master's house, she would probably have starved. Months went by until one morning, as one who awakens from a long and restful sleep, she walked out of her hut smiling broadly. Her face possessed a new radiance, as if a sun had come to rest within her and, eager to shine its brightest, flowed out of her eyes. She took to wandering the streets with no clear destination, apparently deaf to those who spoke to her. It took the villagers several days to realize that she had gone mad.

[Storyteller's note: At this point the bartender interrupted his narrative, leaned forward toward me, and stared directly into my eyes.]

My friend, we fool ourselves into believing that there is a discrete line separating fantasy from reality. There is, in fact, no such line. It could be argued that perhaps, at the extremes, reality and fantasy are well defined. To understand this better, we may use the analogy of day and night; one has no difficulty determining that it is day at noon, or that it's night after midnight. But between the extremes of night and day there is an area of transition, where one flows into the other so that it's neither night nor day, and yet it is both. Between reality and fantasy there is also a twilight of sorts that we all tend to frequent on a daily basis, at times for short intervals, at other times for more prolonged periods. In fact, our everyday life consists of an ever-changing balance of fantasy and reality.

Fantasy and reality are also at times reflections of each other. Consider a man sitting comfortably on a couch staring into his fireplace, his wife and children sleeping soundly upstairs. He is slightly bored and feeling a bit sorry for himself, and he fantasizes about being in a faraway exotic and exciting place. But that same man, if his situation were to change, if he were to find himself in less favorable circumstances…if the next day, for example, he were to find himself unexpectedly in prison, or in a hospital, then he would fantasize about sitting comfortably on a couch, staring into his fireplace, his wife and children sleeping soundly upstairs; so the reality, once boring and routine, would now become the cherished fantasy. Thus the same scene can at one time be real and at another imagined, like two mirror images facing each other.

But there are those individuals, powerful alchemists and magicians, who possess a special talent or skill that enables them to immerse themselves so much in fantasy that they are able to change that fantasy into reality. The common man lacks the ability to penetrate that magic and thus, without assistance, is unable to experience the reality created by the magician; seeing the magician is like seeing a mime run his hands along an invisible wall. Upon observing the magician convincingly play a role on an invisible stage, the common man may assume that the magician is in fact mentally deranged. But this is of no consequence to the magician, who, within his or her fantasy world, has no time or special concern for disbelievers. And to many of those magicians, for whom reality holds no trace of kindness or hope, fantasy and madness are modes of salvation. Many times also, some of the magician's best work is performed secretly and unobserved.

[Storyteller's note: The bartender now sat back on his stool and calmly resumed his story.]

One afternoon during her wanderings Soledad came upon a plastic doll lying beside the road. A few hours earlier, a crying child resisting being dragged home by her mother had dropped the doll in defiance, but her frustrated mother had not looked back. So the doll lay abandoned on the ground with eyes closed, its face radiating an air of peace, as if awaiting a more deserving mission than that of being the plaything of a spoiled and stubborn child.

When she came upon the doll, Soledad stood looking at it as if in a trance. So realistic were the doll's features that at first she thought it was a sleeping infant six to eight months of age. When she realized it was just a doll, she picked it up and tenderly held it to her chest. But then she straightened up as if struck by a sudden realization and looked around her with frightened eyes, fearful that the doll would be snatched away from her; but there was nobody to be seen. And then Soledad did something that came upon her as an impulse from a deep and mysterious place. She lifted the doll's face to her own and blew into its nostrils, and the doll child came to life in her eyes!

From that moment on Soledad was never seen without the doll. She clothed it, sang it to sleep, and gently and lovingly nudged it in the morning to awaken it from its night's rest. The doll became the child that had been so ruthlessly taken away from her. And the loneliness that had enveloped her for so many years suddenly lifted. The villagers seemed initially perplexed by Soledad's strange behavior. Some of them were amused and broke out laughing when she walked by, tenderly holding her toy child. But surprisingly, most of the villagers were overtaken by a strange sense of sadness and compassion for that woman who was so desperately lonesome that a rubber doll could serve as her only source of solace.

One evening, when a group of villagers had gathered in a tavern, a usually quiet young man, his tongue perhaps loosened by the cheap alcohol, related with some hesitation a strange event concerning Soledad. A few days before he had stood by her outside a store, waiting for it to open. They did not speak to each other, and Soledad's attention seemed totally devoted to the toy doll that she held in her arms. She talked to it as she usually did, cooing to it as if it were a real baby. The villager related that he almost fell to the ground in amazement when he heard a cry, like that of a real child, coming from the doll.

The silence that ensued after the villager told his story bore proof to the surprise experienced by the rest of the group upon hearing it. They seemed unsure as to whether the young man was joking, or was indeed serious. The young man looked around the silent room and sank into his seat, withdrawing into his drink, as if feeling remorse for having somehow exposed himself through the telling of his strange story.

Some of the villagers broke the silence and began questioning him, their tone of voice midway between amusement and curiosity. Perhaps he had too much to drink that day, one of them suggested, but the young man replied that he had tasted no alcohol. Maybe it was his imagination playing tricks on him said another; but he angrily replied that he was not a man prone to dreams or hallucinations. And when more questions were posed to him, the exasperated young man angrily stormed out of the bar. In truth, he found it difficult to defend the veracity of an event that he himself was not able to fully believe or comprehend.

Strangely enough, the villagers did not break out laughing upon his departure. Instead, a profound silence, perhaps stemming from shame, once more took hold of the room. And then, one of the older villagers, a man highly respected for his wisdom and common sense, broke the silence.

"Perhaps what he said is true. Perhaps the doll that Soledad carries did indeed cry out," he said. The statement took the villagers by surprise. An energetic dialog ensued among them. How could that be? How could a plastic doll cry? The old man held his ground. "Not everything that can be seen is readily visible to the eye," he argued. During the course of his long life, he had been witness to many mysterious events. He confessed that on one occasion, during a particularly taxing time in his life, when he was so much weighed down by life that he had wished for death, he had gone to the jungle to await his own passing. He walked for hours, and when exhausted he leaned on a giant tree to rest. An owl landed on a nearby branch. The bird talked to the old man at length, and what he told him so much encouraged him that for the first time in many years he desired to go on living.

The group of villagers, most with lightened hearts and minds from the abundant alcohol, listened intently to the old man's tale. And gradually, albeit with a certain degree of trepidation, as if revealing a deep and hidden secret, each of them recounted an event that had occurred to him, or that he had witnessed, that had questioned his hold on reality. Tales of speaking animals and trees, of a river that slowed its waters to allow an innocent man to escape from his pursuers, of stars that danced in the sky to the music of the wind; their tales filled the room with light and shadows, creating images on faces and walls. And when later that night the young man returned to the bar expecting to find it empty, he was surprised to find a large group of villagers sitting in a circle, listening to each other. When he turned to leave, expecting the villagers to laugh at him, they instead warmly welcomed him, asking him to join them in the circle.

A short distance from the bar, in a meager shack at the edge of town, a frail and hungry Soledad, softly and lovingly whispering to her plastic doll, would never realize the magic that she had worked among the villagers that night. From that day on all of the people smiled warmly

at her when they passed her on the street, a sharp contrast from the sneers that she had encountered from a
number of them in the past.

At the outskirts of the village there lived an old man in
a house in front of which was a large, fenced-in garden.
Inside the garden were hundreds of clay objects of every shape and form. Figures of winged angels playing
flutes, of unicorns and roaring lions, of bearded old men
sitting with their chins upon their fists, of giant turtles
with laughing children on their backs, seemed to all
come together to create their own magical world. This
strange world inhabited by the strangest of figures was
perhaps the only attraction for the infrequent tourists
who passed through the town. They would enter the
garden, quickly walk its paths, marvel at the variety of
the menagerie, and very occasionally purchase one of
the figures.

One early afternoon, while the old man sat on a chair
propped up against a wall of his house, his eyes half
open and his mind somewhere between wakefulness
and sleep, he saw Soledad standing at the garden gate.
As usual, she held the plastic doll in her arms, slightly
rocking from side to side. She looked at the old man
pleadingly, as if asking for his permission to enter. The
old man, now fully awake, looked at Soledad curiously.
He had heard much about this strange woman who could

make plastic dolls cry. And then, without rising from his chair, he made a quick gesture with his hand, as if inviting Soledad to enter the garden.

By this time Soledad had lost the power of speech. Her mouth emitted only a few grunts when she was particularly excited, or when she felt overly happy or sad. And as she walked along the paths of the garden, she marveled at the figures as though she had discovered a world of treasures. Every once in a while she would kneel next to a particular statue and make a sound of delight, as would a child upon seeing a beautiful and precious toy. When she came upon the figure of a dog she almost seemed to gasp for air, so great was her excitement. She put out her hand and gently patted the statue's head, as if it were a real animal, and then she placed the plastic doll's hand on the animal's head. The doll cried out in bliss.

The joyous giggles made by Soledad attracted the attention of the old man, who almost grudgingly arose from his chair and approached the woman. Soledad, startled by his presence, quickly stood up and took a few steps backwards, clutching the doll in her arms. They looked into each other's eyes for several seconds, and the old man saw sadness and beauty, loneliness and refuge, resignation and hope. And suddenly, possessed by an emotion somewhere between admiration, understanding and compassion, he grabbed the dog statue and handed it to Soledad, urging her to take it. She smiled at him, and clutching the dog statue under her left arm and the doll on the opposite arm, she walked out of the garden. The farmer followed her with his eyes until she disappeared from sight; then he shook his head as though in disbelief and returned to his chair.

When Soledad arrived home she lovingly put the doll in the crib that she had rescued from a garbage dump. She then took the dog statue in her arms and blew into its nostrils. And the statue, suddenly liberated from the clay cage that had imprisoned it for so many years, came to life in Soledad's eyes. With gratitude the animal licked her hand, as she held it lovingly.

Only once did Soledad return to the garden, and that was several months after her initial visit. As she had done before, she stood at the gate until the old man invited her in. She then walked directly over to the center of the garden, where stood a statue of two opposing cherubs. They held their hands in the air, as if dancing, with broad smiles on their faces. Soledad looked pleadingly at the old man, and he lifted the statue from the ground and handed it to her. So broad was her smile of gratitude that it lit up the old man's heart.

Again, as she had done with the plastic doll and the dog of clay, Soledad blew the breath of life into the angels' nostrils. That night, so joyously did the cherubs sing and dance in the miserable shack, that the laugh of the toy child in his crib seemed as a precious stream endlessly flowing down a mountain, and the dog was unable to contain his happiness and jumped from side to side as though he himself were dancing.

Soledad, her heart overflowing with gratitude and happiness, was suddenly overcome by a profound and peaceful tiredness. She took the baby from the crib and, embracing it in her arms, lay down on the bed and closed her eyes. The dog also climbed up on the bed, turned about to find a comfortable spot, and fell asleep next to the infant. And the two cherubs stopped their dancing, and standing on each side of the bed, softly sang with angelic voices until Soledad and the baby fell asleep. Then they lay down one on each side of Soledad's head, and with smiles on their beautiful faces, also fell fast asleep.

And that is how they found her the next day: dead, with a smile on her face, embracing the "sleeping" toy doll. The dog and cherubs looked so serene and real that the villagers who saw them thought they appeared more to be sleeping than mere statues of clay. The villagers placed the toy and the statues in the coffin in which Soledad was buried.

Among the small group attending the funeral was the same young man who had told the story of the crying baby doll. He did not clearly understand his reasons for attending the burial, but the previous night as he had returned home from the bar, his senses somewhat distorted by the alcohol that he had consumed earlier, he had heard the most beautiful of songs emanating from Soledad's shack. And intermingled with the almost angelic voices of children singing, he had also heard the happy barking of a dog.

The young man, his heart troubled by a lifetime of futile searching for meaning, of years of drinking in an attempt to drown painful memories, of remorse for a mistake made many years before, of longing for the most beautiful of loves that he had allowed to pass as a shipwrecked man on an island allows a saving ship to pass by; that young man, intoxicated and devoid of all hope, had sat on a tree stump a few feet from Soledad's home and listened to that music that seemed to originate from heaven itself. And with every note his burdened heart had become lighter. For the first time in decades he had felt happiness and peace. And what else other than happiness and peace could a man want? When the music ended, he had walked away, a free man at last. A few days after the funeral, he left the town forever.

[Storyteller's note: "Another fabulous story," I said. "I assume it is only a story? Again, if it were true, I would be at a loss as to how you would know all this!" The bartender stared at me in that intense way of his. "But you still do not understand my establishment, do you?

SILENT SINNERS, SILENT SAINTS

Let me explain things a bit more directly.

"Truth and meaning are not the same, despite what scientists, theologians, and other 'great thinkers' often believe, and try to make us believe. Here in my bar, they are the same. That is why it seems so strange to you. Usually, when an event occurs, when it happens for all to see and thus is declared 'true,' the meaning of that event nevertheless remains hidden. Not so here! That is why the stories that have been told to you today did indeed seem so 'meaningful.' There are few places where such telling can be accomplished- the world prevents such revelations and we remain a mystery to ourselves (because, you see, while truth is shared, meaning is always personal). Where can such self-realization occur? Where can we begin to come to ourselves? Only here. And the realization comes, if not to the teller, then to others, but only through the telling. The people you met today were drawn here by a need, just as were you. Their need was to tell, yours to listen. But the tremendous spiritual and mental power required to bring us all here in this place came from one source alone. Do not worry, you will find your sister. She would not have it any other way! Now go. Return home and write what you have experienced."

"But," I stammered, "Who are you? What did all of this mean?"

He smiled. "Consider all that you have seen and heard today, and I think you will realize who I am and why you were called here. Your family and mine have been linked for a very long time now. My younger brother aided your sister with his magic; now I aid you, along with all those who took part today, with my much stronger magic."

With that, the bartender winked, turned, and ambled out of the bar. It was then that I realized, "My God! He walks with a limp!"]

THE END